The New Christian's Field Guide

The New Christian's Field Guide

52 Weeks of Essential Topics

Compiled by Joseph Dindinger

ILLUMINATION PUBLISHERS INTERNATIONAL
www.ipibooks.com

The New Christian's Field Guide
52 Weeks of Essential Topics

© 2009 by Joseph Dindinger

ISBN: 978-0-9842006-4-1

All rights reserved. No part of this book may be duplicated, copied, translated, reproduced or stored mechanically or electronically without specific, written permission of Joseph Dindinger and Illumination Publishers International.

Printed in the United States of America

All scripture quotations unless otherwise indicated are taken from the NEW INTERNATIONAL VERSION. Copyright © 1973, 1978, 1984 by the International Bible Society. Used by permission of Zondervan Publishing House. All rights reserved.

The "NIV" and "New International Version" trademarks are registered in the United States Patent Trademark Office by the International Bible Society. Use of either trademark requires the permission of the International Bible Society.

INTERIOR AND COVER DESIGN BY:
CHRISTIAN VALLEJOS, JAMES DONVITO, NICOLE MENCARINI AND PAUL HAGERTY

Published by
Illumination Publishers International
6010 Pinecreek Ridge Court
Spring, Texas 77379
www.ipibooks.com

Dedicated to:

Jay and Traci Minor, whose passion for new disciples inspired this book.

The entire Faith21.org team, without whom this effort would not have been possible.

Foreword

Our mission as a church is to move people toward Christ. Our dream is to be used by God to change thousands of lives as we build a healthy church that lasts for generations. This book represents a collaborative effort toward that end. It contains wisdom gained by 35 Christians of every background and is designed to impart their hard-won perspectives to our newest generation of disciples.

This work is a source of deep encouragement to us because it is indicative of a core conviction we hold in the Turning Point: every disciple is valuable, insightful, helpful and necessary. We're better together! Each one of us is called on by God to make our spiritual mark in our church family and in the world. Faith21 has embraced the "you're it" ministry concept and has launched this process. This ministry is not staff driven but member driven because "every member is a minister."

It is the honor of a lifetime to be a part of this community of faith. Our sentiment about the writers specifically and the Turning Point in general is reflected in Paul's encouragement to the church in Rome when he said:

> "For myself, I feel certain that you, my brothers, have real Christian character and experience, and that you are capable of keeping each other on the right road."
>
> Romans 15:14 (J. B. Phillips)

Hopefully, this resource will educate, inspire and encourage you in your Christian journey. As with everything you read, ask questions, seek answers, let God teach you new things and strive to grow deeper as you build your spiritual foundation on the Word of God. Have the ride of your life and enjoy every God moment!

All our love and God's best to you,

Kevin and Tracena Holland
Senior Minister and Women's Ministry Leader
Turning Point Christian Church
Los Angeles, California
www.turningpointla.com

Contents

Letter to the Reader   1

Section One
Fundamentals of Christianity

1 **God**— Images Of The Indescribable   5
2 **The Holy Spirit**— May The Force Be With You   10
3 **Jesus**— Follow The Leader   15
4 **Return Of The King**— Living In Expectation Of Christ's Return   20
    Christian Conundrums— The End Times   25
5 **Grace vs. Works**— Growing In The Light Of Grace   26
6 **The Sovereignty Of God**— Who Is In Control Here?   31
7 **Who Is Saved?**— Salvation Yesterday, Today And Tomorrow   36
    Christian Conundrums— HELL   41
8 **Hell**— Abandon All Hope, You Who Enter Here   42
9 **Heaven**— Great Expectations   48

Section Two
Discipleship: Becoming Like Jesus

10 **Prayer**— Can We Talk?   55
11 **Mmm… God's Word!**— Our Daily Bread   60
12 **Let It Go**— What Should I Leave Behind?   65
13 **Let Them Go**— Whom Should I Leave Behind?   70
14 **Balance**— It Is A Marathon, Not A Sprint   75

15	**God's Discipline**— Considering It Pure Joy	81
16	**Openness**— Walking In The Light	86
17	**Accountability**— You Can't Go It Alone	91
18	**Victory!**— Against All Odds	96
19	**Sexual Purity**— Overcoming A Multi-Faced Sin	101
20	**Spiritual Warfare**— There's A Target On Your Back	107
21	**Financial Stewardship**— Whose Money Is It Anyway?	113
22	**Generosity**— It Is Better To Give Than To Receive	118
23	**Living Sacrifice**— Giving Up Everything For Jesus	123
24	**Pride**— The Hidden Killer	128
25	**Deep Healing**— God Longs To Heal Your Heart	133
	Christian Conundrums— Why Did Jesus Die?	139
26	**Love**— The Greatest Commandment	140
27	**Born Identity**— I Know Whose I Am	145
28	**Sowing And Reaping**— Pulling Up The Roots	150
29	**Life To The Full**— Where Is This Life We Are Promised?	155
30	**Finding Your Shape**— Exploring Your Unique Purpose	160

Section Three
One Another

31	**The Kingdom**— Where Jesus Is King	167
32	**Church History**— How Did We Get Here?	172
33	**Worship**— A Way Of Life	178
34	**Fellowship**— Do I Really Need To Be Connected?	183
35	**Creating Family**— Life In A Small Group	188
36	**Conflict Resolution**— Doing It God's Way	193
37	**Christian Dating**— It Isn't Just About Finding A Spouse	198

38 **Finding That Special One**— What To Do While Waiting	203
39 **Marriage**— The Roles God Designed Us To Play	208
40 **Parenting**— Respecting Our Children	213

Section Four
Sharing the Light

41 **Evangelism**— Fishing With A Purpose And A Plan	221
42 **Shining Like Stars**— And If You Must, Use Words	226
43 **Respecting Authority**— As Unto The Lord	231
44 **Excellence At Work**— God Is Your Boss	237
45 **Relatability**— Understanding And Reaching Those Around Us	242
Christian Conundrums— War	247
46 **Firestorm!**— Persecution In Our New Lives	248
47 **Other Churches**— Are We Alone In Our Christianity?	253
Christian Conundrums— Politics	259
48 **Moral Relativism**— Do All Roads Lead To Rome?	260
49 **Humanism**— Does Man Control His Own Destiny?	265
50 **Atheism**— Does God Exist?	271
51 **Science And The Bible**— Where Do We Come From?	276
Christian Conundrums— How Did We Get Here?	281
52 **Social Justice**— And As You Read This…	282
The Rest of the Journey	288
Our Story: Author Listing	290

Letter to the Reader

Dear Friend,

  If you can tell, I've gotten some good use out of this old book. It was given to me long ago by an older disciple and is filled with lessons collected over the years from brothers and sisters who have gone before us in the Way.

  In order to get the most out of this book, I recommend four things:

1. Read one chapter per week. The chapters are short, but slowing down will really
help to move the topics from your head into your heart.

2. Ask an older brother or sister to help you through these topics. Meet together each week and discuss the questions you find at the end of each chapter. This exercise will prove invaluable to you.

3. Each chapter will have additional scriptures that you can look up for your own study. I recommend you look up all of the scriptures referenced. You can also use the resources at the end of each chapter to gain a deeper understanding. However, as with any

book, please pray for discernment as you read (I Thessalonians 5:21).

4. Finally, please take the challenges for growth listed at the end of each chapter. I have found that we often cannot learn something fully until we put it into practice.

As you start to read, you may notice that this book is far from a literary masterpiece; it was written by dozens of simple Christians, just like you and me. Some of the chapters were penned by evangelists and church leaders; others by teachers, factory workers, horse dentists and starving artists. The only thing that joins all of them and us together is the love we share for Jesus Christ.

The insight and encouragement I received from this book have been invaluable to me over the years. I have learned from others to grow through my struggles, to become more faithful through life's lessons and to always keep the example of our Lord before me as I draw nearer to God the Father. I hope and pray that it will help you do the same.

With love in our common Lord,
An Anonymous Christian

P.S. Do me a favor: when another young Christian comes your way, pass this book along.

Section One
Fundamentals of Christianity

The following nine chapters cover topics that every Christian should be well acquainted with. They will set a foundation for everything you learn going forward in your walk with God.

You are babies, new-born in God's family, and you should be crying out for unadulterated spiritual milk to make you grow up to salvation! And so you will, if you have already tasted the goodness of the Lord.

I Peter 2:2-3 (J.B. Phillips)

1

God
Images of the Indescribable

> *Who is like the LORD our God, the One who sits enthroned on high, who stoops down to look on the heavens and the earth?*
>
> Psalm 113:5-6

When we first study the Bible, an amazing thing happens: our skewed vision of God begins to transform. It is something akin to going to the eye doctor to have your vision checked. As you sit looking at the eye chart, with its lines of letters in ever-decreasing sizes, the doctor pulls over a large machine equipped with a set of lenses to look through. At first, the letters are still unclear. But slowly, as the doctor tries lens after lens, the letters start to become clearer and clearer, until eventually, you are able to see with amazing clarity those letters that just minutes before were nothing more than ink splotches. In the same way, when we first study the Bible, our vision of God is fuzzy and vague, if not completely absent. For some, the "god" we see isn't even close to the real image of God. Yet, as we read the Bible, pray and seek God with all of our hearts, he adjusts our vision. Somehow, like a doctor, he corrects our vision, bringing into focus even the minute and intricate details of his character. We begin to see that the true God of the Bible looks nothing like we imagined him.

If our image of God was previously aloof and austere, we begin to see his tenderness and his attention to the intimate details of our lives (Matthew 10:29-31). A previously harsh and condemning image changes into a view of a God full of compassion and abounding in love (Psalm 103). A wimpy, powerless image becomes a powerful warrior God, mighty and ready to save (Psalm 18). Scripture after scripture, day after day, year after year, our spiritual eyes become more focused and we see God with more clarity.

As we read about God in his love letter to us, the Bible, we get to read beautiful stories of how he has repeatedly come through for his people. We also get to see how he describes himself—the creator, the potter, the father, the lover, the friend, the husband. These are the descriptions he chooses. God refers to himself as the Alpha and Omega, or the beginning and the end, in Revelation. To Moses, he is revealed as the "I AM." These descriptions of God are so perfect because God is who he needs to be for every person, in every situation, at any point in time. Are you in need of protection? He is your refuge. Are you in need of understanding? He is full of compassion. Are you in need of a father? He is the only perfect parent. Have you been abandoned? He will never leave you. Are you in need of character development? He will train you. God is the perfect answer to every question and the perfect fulfillment of every need. He knows our hearts and understands what we truly desire even more than we do. Chris Tomlin, a Christian singer, puts it this way:

> *A refuge for the poor*
> *A shelter from the storm*
> *This is our God.*

He will wipe away your tears
and return your wasted years
This is our God.
A father to the orphan
A healer to the broken
This is our God.
He brings peace to our madness
and comfort in our sadness
This is our God.
A fountain for the thirsty
A lover for the lonely
This is our God.
He brings glory to the humble
and crowns for the faithful
This is our God.

There truly is no one like the Lord. Yet, as we go about living here in our fallen state, surrounded by imperfect people and struggling to make sense of the mess we have often made of our lives, it can sometimes be difficult to connect with God in our hearts, even though our brains remind us of all his benefits. It is in those times that we learn that our new "spiritual vision" is still in need of adjustment. We find blind spots or spiritual astigmatisms. Even though we know that the Bible says God is compassionate, it doesn't feel like it. Our head knowledge doesn't match up with our heart and we begin to wonder if God really is all that he says he is. It is in those times that we need to be reminded that God can be trusted. He is the same yesterday, today and forever. It is only our perspective that must be altered.

I still remember going through a very tough spell in my early years as a Christian. Life was hard, I was confused and I couldn't see God clearly. It was then that a wonderful mentor of mine gave me the following exercise. I was challenged to write out I Corinthians 13:4-7, substituting God's name for the word "love":

> **God** is patient. **God** is kind. **God** does not envy. **God** does not boast. **God** is not proud. **God** is not rude. **God** is not self-seeking. **God** is not easily angered. **God** keeps no record of wrongs. **God** does not delight in evil but rejoices with the truth. **God** always protects. **God** always trusts. **God** always hopes. **God** always perseveres.

I wrote down each phrase individually, then followed it by answering whether I truly believed it or not. For example, I really had no problem believing that "God is kind," but "God is patient"...well, not so much! It was then that I started to realize that my God image was out of focus. I wasn't seeing him as he truly is. There were many reasons: my relationship with my dad, my own unhealthy expectations of myself and previous religious experiences to name a few. Regardless of the reasons, I needed a spiritual vision adjustment. This exercise helped me to break through many blind spots of which I wasn't even aware. I highly recommend it for anyone truly interested in breaking through their own vision limitations in order to see God more clearly.

There truly is no greater question than "Who is like the LORD?" For centuries, poets, songwriters, sages and theologians have tried to put God into words, endeavoring to describe all of his benefits and character traits; but truly, who could do him justice? For God is so complex, so intricate, so infinitely beyond description, no one could even come close to conveying his wonder and beauty. Yet this is the God who wants us to know him and who wants to know us.

GOD: Images of the Indescribable

Stuff to Talk Through With a Friend
* Go through the exercise listed in the text above; share your findings. Ask:
* What are some scriptures I can use to help me understand that God is _____? (Whatever attribute it is you need help with)
* Are there any Old Testament stories or characters that can help me to understand this attribute of God?
* What helps you to trust God in this area of your life?

Things to Do If You Want to Grow
* Reread I Corinthians 13. Describe the ways God is the same and different from your earthly father.
* Go on a "date" with God, just you and him, away from distractions. Ask him to reveal more of his nature to you. Focus the time on listening and watching for what he wants to show you about himself.
* Take the time to go through the exercise above in one of your quiet times this week.

References for Further Bible Study
Job 38:1-41:34 • Psalm 77:1-20, 86, 89, 91, 93, 103, 104, 107, 113, 139 • Exodus 3:13-15 • Revelation 21:22-23, 22:4-5, 22:12-13

Additional Resources
The Attributes of God, Volumes 1 & 2 by A. W. Tozer
The Divine Romance by Gene Edwards
Our God Is an Awesome God ed. by Kelly and Dede Petre
Desire by John Eldredge

For additional resources or to join our online community, go to:
http://fieldguide.faith21.org

2

The Holy Spirit
May the Force Be with You

> *"But the Counselor, the Holy Spirit, whom the Father will send in my name, will teach you all things and will remind you of everything I have said to you. Peace I leave with you; my peace I give you. I do not give to you as the world gives. Do not let your hearts be troubled and do not be afraid."*
> John 14:26

Jesus promised peace to his disciples because he knew that much of their lives would be spent fighting a spiritual battle. As young Christians, the battle is very clear. Our old ways and desires continually try to pull us back to the life we used to have. As we grow in our faith and convictions, the battle enters a new, even more dangerous, deeper level. Over the years, we will see victory after victory, yet there will also be many casualties along the way. Many friends will leave God and lose the battle, along with their faith. This chapter is about the only power that can keep you from being a casualty in this war.

One of my biggest challenges when I became a Christian was self-reliance, and fifteen years later, it remains my biggest battle. Only now have I begun to understand the cost of my self-reliance. The power that parted the Red Sea and raised Jesus from the dead was given to me (Romans 8:11), and yet my life says, "No thanks, I don't need it." It's a ludicrous way to live. When Christ ascended into Heaven, he left the Holy Spirit for us, the Counselor, to be with us always (John 14:16-17).

When we rely on our own strength, we grieve the Holy Spirit. Ephesians 4:30 (The Message) says, "Don't grieve God. Don't break his heart. His Holy Spirit, moving and breathing in you, is the most intimate part of your life, making you fit for himself. Don't take such a gift for granted." As Andrew Murray, a 19th-century minister and writer, points out, "The Holy Spirit is meant to be in us and through us so that all the action of the heart, all that is done by it, is done by the Holy Spirit inspiring it."[1]

How do we grieve the Holy Spirit? We grieve him by beginning our day without turning it over to God in prayer. We grieve him by worrying and being anxious and by taking that out on the people around us. The Bible teaches that the Kingdom of God is righteousness, peace and joy (Romans 14:17-18). If that is what the Holy Spirit is offering, why would we ignore him?

Christ's presence is here with us in the form of the Holy Spirit. Jesus said that the Spirit was even nearer to the twelve disciples than he could be in the flesh (John 16:7). "The abiding nearness and fellowship of Christ, and of God the Father through him, is the very central blessing of the Kingdom."[2] When we enter into the Kingdom, we have chosen a life where God is to rule over all. When God's will is truly and joyfully done, we are able to experience some of the blessedness that reigns in Heaven. We must believe that here on Earth we can have such a life.

The problem with relying on our own strength is that it

---

1 Andrew Murray, *On The Holy Spirit*, (New Kensington, PA: Whitaker House, 1998).
2 ibid.

gives out quickly; and when it does, Satan is given a foothold. On our own strength, we cannot withstand the relentless attacks of Satan. We cannot fight the good fight of faith without the Holy Spirit. God knows that and he gave us his Spirit for exactly that reason. On the day of Pentecost, the Holy Spirit brought the Kingdom of God into the hearts of the disciples (Acts 2). This same power has been passed on to each succeeding generation at conversion.

How difficult it is for men and women, with our wills and our strength and our wisdom, to have the humble heart of a child so we may truly receive the Kingdom of Heaven. "The mind of a sinful man is death, but the mind controlled by the Spirit is life and peace" (Romans 8:6)! In order to fully trust in God, give up our rights and surrender to him, we must first know God enough to truly rest in his innate goodness. When we live in our fears, we cannot find freedom in God's love. Our independence, with its quest for power and fulfillment, actually destroys the relationship our heart longs for. However, when we are connected and surrendered to God, submission to him is the most natural expression of that relationship (Galatians 3:3-5). As Andrew Murray puts it:

> "If you are not living in the joy of his salvation, the entire cause is your unbelief. Fix your desire; fix your heart on his grace. Do not let any thoughts of your unworthiness or shortcomings discourage you. Do you believe as definitely and naturally in the indwelling Spirit? Is it one of the elements of your faith as truly as you believe in Christ crucified? It is only as this truth is accepted and held fast that the others can truly benefit you. If you find your spiritual life to be weak and powerless, it is because you do not know, really know that Christ is in YOU."[3]

---

3 Andrew Murray, On The Holy Spirit, (New Kensington, PA: Whitaker House, 1998).

Christ came to this Earth and showed us the possibility of being a man in whom God is living his life (Galatians 2:20-21). Understanding the Holy Spirit and his power in your life will only come through true surrender. Pray every day to surrender your will and then watch God carry you where he wants you to go. It may even turn out to be the destination you have always desired. When you truly understand and experience the power of God, then all fear will vanish, even fear of Satan (Ephesians 3:16-19)!

THE HOLY SPIRIT:
May the Force Be with You

Stuff to Talk Through With a Friend
* What is stopping you from truly surrendering your will over to God? What are your fears?
* What is your current belief or understanding about the Holy Spirit?
* What kind of power do you realize you already have with this knowledge of the Holy Spirit?
* Confess your self-will and self-effort. Talk about it. Describe your battles so your friends can pray for you and with you.

Things to Do If You Want to Grow
* Do a study on the Holy Spirit. Look up every scripture on it. You'll be amazed!
* Pray specifically for God to expose anything that might be stopping you from truly surrendering your life over to him.
* Pray and strive for a child-like spirit to rely on and trust in God.
* Re-read the entire book of Acts. See how the Spirit came with power and completely changed the apostles into powerful men of God.

References for Further Bible Study
Romans 8 • Acts 2 • John 14 (esp. 15-31); 16:1-6 • Hebrews 13:20-21 • II Peter 1:21 • Ephesians chapters 4-6

Additional Resources
On the Holy Spirit by Andrew Murray
The Power of the Spirit by William Law (edited by Dave Hunt)
The Spirit by Douglas Jacoby
The Holy Spirit: From Genesis to Pentecost by Andrew Fleming

For additional resources or to join our online community, go to:
http://fieldguide.faith21.org

3

Jesus
Follow the Leader

"The virgin will be with child and will give birth to a son, and they will call him 'Immanuel'—which means, 'God with us.'"
Matthew 1:23

What would cause a rational person to change his or her life to follow a man who:
* lived more than two thousand years ago
* was little more than an itinerant preacher
* was arrested, convicted and executed by the Roman Empire?

Crucifixion was an especially terrible form of execution which was normally reserved for slaves, rebels and the most heinous criminals, so why would anyone in their right minds make a man who died this way Lord of their lives? How much do we really even know of this Jesus of Nazareth?

Many religious and secular sources indicate that Jesus lived in the first-century Holy Land (modern-day Israel). The writers of the New Testament attest to Jesus' life. The first-century church, which spread quickly across the known world, was moved by him. Early Christians lived for him and early martyrs died for him. Josephus, Tacitus and Pliny the Younger are a few of the most important extra-biblical sources who mention Christ and his followers. Even most non-Christian critics do not doubt that Jesus lived, though they discount the idea that he was the Son of God.

The divinity of the man Jesus is of utmost importance; in fact, it is at the core of Christian belief. The beginning of the Gospel of John reads, "In the beginning was the Word, and the Word was with God, and the Word was God...The Word became flesh and made his dwelling among us" (John 1:1, 14). If the man Jesus is not also God, then Christianity would be little more than idolatry. We can, as thousands before us have, meditate on the person of Jesus and attempt to figure out the mystery of how Jesus was both at the same time God and man, both human and divine. This is a worthy endeavor, but perhaps a secondary matter to those new in the faith. What is also very important for Christians to understand, new Christians in particular, is not only the fact *that* Jesus lived or *who* Jesus was, but *how* Jesus lived.

First, Jesus is both the Son of God and our high priest "who has been tempted in every way, just as we are—yet was without sin" (Hebrews 4:15). In spite of his holy position, Jesus has given us the ability to "approach the throne of grace with confidence, so that we may receive mercy and find grace to help us in our time of need" (Hebrews 4:16). But it is not only for the greater theological concept that Jesus is God that he has drawn so many to him. Jesus' crucifixion was the final sacrifice for our sins and his resurrection guarantees God's victory over Satan, sin and death. Jesus is Immanuel, "God with us"; thus, his words and deeds from the time of his birth to his ascension to heaven are of utmost importance.

Second, as the beginning and the head of the Church, Jesus set the example of how we should live. As the living example of good news for the poor, the hungry and the suffering, Jesus works to liberate all people. Jesus attracts followers to his cause because he healed the sick, fed the hungry and touched the untouchable. The importance of Jesus comes not only from who he is as God, but also from what he did as a human being.

The self-proclaimed Son of Man lived his life with simplicity, yet he helped others live life to the full (John 10:10). He lived his life with humility, yet he was not afraid to confront the heartless and challenge the faithless. Jesus confronted the hypocrisy of the religious elite (Luke 18:9-14). Nothing angered Jesus more than when the children, the needy or the sinful were kept away from him (Matthew 19:13-14; Mark 2:13-17; Matthew 25:41-46). Nothing pleased him more than when his followers tended to the needs of others and were themselves tended to (Matthew 23:13-15, 25:31-40; Luke 9:1-5). Jesus cursed the fig tree, drove the money changers out of the temple and boldly healed the man with the withered hand on the Sabbath (Mark 3:1-6). Though impressively filled with divine power to do such miracles, Jesus had a soft heart and wept when others wept (John 11:33-35). He was close enough to his people that he called them friends (John 15:15). Jesus expects his followers to live their lives in a similar way to how he lived: "A new command I give you: Love one another. As I have loved you, so you must love one another. By this all men will know that you are my disciples, if you love one another" (John 13:34-35).

One of the first things that attracted me to Christianity was the genuine love of Christians for one another. Coming out of a life of pain and loneliness, I immediately doubted the sincerity of the Christians I met. I thought to myself, "There's no way someone can be that outgoing and that selfless and not be hiding something." However, after getting to know various Christians, I discovered that their love was true and this love came about by a conscious effort to imitate the life of Jesus. I was living my life filled with both hate and hurt, but the life of Jesus was filled with joy and love. My life was lived in selfishness; Jesus lived his life in self*less*ness. I lived my life taking what I could get; Jesus lived his life giving all he had. There was no purpose to my life, but Jesus gives purpose—to know and be restored to a relationship with God and one another. Because of Jesus' life and what he has done for humanity, our life is "renewed in knowledge in the image of its Creator." We are now able to rid ourselves of "anger, rage, malice, slander and filthy language" being part of God's chosen people. We must be clothed with "compassion, kindness, humility, gentleness and patience," all of which make up the core of the character of Jesus. We are no longer slaves to sin which wages war in our hearts and minds, but are able to "let the peace of Christ rule in [our] hearts" and "be thankful" (Colossians 3).

JESUS: Follow the Leader

Stuff to Talk Through With a Friend
* When I think of Jesus, what image comes to mind?
* If Jesus came to visit my church today, would he be pleased with what he saw?
* If the answer to the previous question is no, what can I do to make my life and my community more like Jesus?

Things to Do If You Want to Grow
* Write down three characteristics of Jesus that you feel you imitate well. Then, write down three characteristics that you feel you do not imitate well. Live out each of those characteristics—one a day for a week—and talk about the results with a friend.
* Imagine Jesus was on trial today and you were his lawyer. Write out a defense for Jesus based on what you've learned about him personally and through your study. Be prepared to use that defense when someone asks you why you believe.
* Choose a character trait of Jesus which you admire but feel you are lacking, and practice it this week.

References for Further Bible Study
John 3:16 • Isaiah chapters 7 and 8 • Matthew 1:23 • The Gospel of John • I Corinthians 1:24

Additional Resources
Jesus The Same by Charles Edward Jefferson
The Case for Christ by Lee Strobel
Jesus in Contemporary Scholarship by Marcus Borg. This scholarly text covers the course of Jesus scholarship over the last half century.

For additional resources or to join our online community, go to:
http://fieldguide.faith21.org

4

Return of the King
Living in Expectation of Christ's Return

> *"Men of Galilee," they said, "why do you stand here looking into the sky? This same Jesus, who has been taken from you into heaven, will come back in the same way you have seen him go into heaven."*
> **Acts 1:11**

"Mommy, what's wrong with the sky?" asked little Mikey as he stopped playing with his sandbox to watch the pretty but strange happenings above his head. "The clouds look funny!"

"Hmm?" his mother Sarah asked distractedly. "Do you see animals in the clouds?"

"I don't think they're animals, mommy, but they do have wings."

"What?" Just as Sarah was about to turn away from her weeding to see what was intriguing her son, a loud noise pierced the atmosphere. It wasn't noise at all. It was music, startling, but beautiful. A verse from an old hymn popped into her mind: *"the trump shall resound and the Lord shall descend..."* Sarah was startled but then an involuntary surge of peace overtook her soul and she whipped her gaze heavenward in time to see him! She couldn't believe her eyes and yet believed them with all her heart at the same time! There he was, descending, just as he said he would! Sarah could see in her peripheral vision, or was she only aware of the host of beings surrounding him as though they were indeed holding back the clouds rolled back like scrolls. He's returned! The air around her seemed to stop flowing, but she was still breathing it in and out. It was as if all time and nature had stopped to gaze at and take it all in. Were those trees actually bowing? Sarah forced her gaze back to the Lord, refusing to be distracted by the strange but prophesied things going on in nature at this moment. She smiled at him and happily bowed low. He smiled in return. Mikey smiled at the "nice man" coming on the "pretty clouds," imitating his mother's bow. Sarah felt as though Christ was looking only at her but she knew better. The King had returned and he had come to gather all of his people, including her and Mikey, unto himself!

Mere words will not be able to describe the experience of every Christian at that moment when Jesus does return to Earth. All of us will see his return (Acts 1:9-11), Christians and non-Christians alike.

First-century believers lived with the hope that the Lord would return in their lifetime (I Corinthians 7:29-31). Though the Bible clearly says no one knows the hour of Jesus' return, people today, as well as back then, show signs of anticipation through eager speculation. Google "Second Coming" and a host of articles will be returned, where people are using today's political and natural events to predict his coming. In spite of the Biblical position that the time of Jesus' second coming is unknown, some people and websites even go so far as to give an exact date—month, day and year—when he is expected. These claims are dubious at best because, no matter what is going on, no one will be able to pinpoint that day; Jesus himself said that not even he knew it (Matthew 24:36). Yet one of the great mysteries of Christianity is that we are to live as though his return is imminent just as our brothers and sisters from the first century did without a specific date and time for his arrival. When we consider the primitive Christian Church, this expectation colored every facet of their collective life and was the ultimate influence on their thoughts, actions, values and priorities. So should it be with us.

If you knew for certain that Jesus was due to return in a manner of weeks, how would it affect your behavior? Some of the early Christians quit their jobs to spread the good news to as many as possible since they believed his return to be right around the corner. I think that we would agree that it would be imprudent to quit your job and become a professional door-knocking, itinerant evangelist. However, a belief that Jesus is coming back, perhaps in our lifetime on Earth, should spur us on to holy living, give us unequaled courage and dynamically increase our evangelism efforts.

The Apostle Paul's directives regarding holy living are that believers must set their hearts and minds on things above. As a believer, you died and your life is now hidden with Jesus in God. As a disciple of Christ, living a life that is holy, you must no longer go with the whims of your earthly nature. Paul lists them as sexual immorality, impurity, lust, evil desire and greed, which he calls idolatry (Colossians 3:1-5). Can you imagine coming face-to-face with the Lord the day after you've committed adultery or even completely ignored an opportunity to profess your faith? The rest of Colossians 3 through 4:6 continues to list holy living rules that include things you should do as a Christian; having a holy household, being devoted to prayer, being watchful and thankful. Living a holy life includes setting yourself apart from the things of the world (John 17:14). Remember that you are not of this world (John 17:16), so don't live as such (Hebrews 13:5). Work as working for the Lord (Colossians 3:23); grow in the knowledge of God (Romans 11:30; Ephesians 4:13; Colossians 1:10); spend time in his presence (I John 3:19; Proverbs 8:30); give to the poor (Hebrews 13:16); and take care of widows (James 1:27). Take time to learn what these things mean and find small ways to obediently apply them to your life. Doing this could take a year's worth of quiet times, but what a foundation you'll have for later years!

Two other effects of living as though he is coming back in our lifetime are living courageously and evangelizing fervently. The phrase "live as though there is no tomorrow" has a negative connotation in our culture. From a Christian's point of view, however, one should live for God as if there is no tomorrow. There may not be one for you (Matthew 13:32), but even if there is, who's to say the person next door will not die tomorrow? God cares for the salvation of all souls (I Timothy 2:4). When the Lord returns, our time is up (John 9:4). In the meantime, have courage, live for him with all your heart (Colossians 3:17) and fear not (I Peter 3:14; Isaiah 41:10, 13), for the Lord is, and always will be, with you (Matthew 28:18-20), now and forever, Amen.

RETURN OF THE KING:
Living in Expectation of Christ's Return

Stuff to Talk Through With a Friend
* What are your areas of strength for holy living?
* What are your areas of weakness?
* What else on Paul's Colossians list may give you trouble in the future?
* Where do you think your courage quotient is regarding reaching out to the lost at this time.

Things to Do If You Want to Grow
* Thank God for the areas where you have strength and reach out to another brother/sister you know is falling short in this area.
* Confess what your weaknesses are and pray about what action should be taken to change/repent.
* Pray daily for the fruit of the Spirit and for the Holy Spirit to help you not take your life in Christ for granted.
* Begin sharing your life in Christ with the people around you, as if you only had one more day.

References for Further Bible Study
Matthew 5:5, 6:9-10, 24:14-44, 25:31-34 • Luke 13:29-30, 21:29-31 • John 14:2-3 • Romans 11:25-26 • Philippians 3:20 • I Timothy 6:14-15 • II Timothy 4:8 • Revelations 1:7

Additional Resources
The Second Coming of Jesus by M. R. De Haan
TheReturnOfJesus.com

For additional resources or to join our online community, go to:
http://fieldguide.faith21.org

CHRISTIAN CONUNDRUMS
The End Times

Eschatology is the study of the prophecies concerning the second coming of Christ and the end of the world. Over the centuries, three main theories have emerged to explain the "1000 years" prophecied in Revelation 20.

Three Eschatological Theories
1. **Amillenial** – A theory that declares the "end" to mean the completion of the Old Covenant by Jesus' first coming and the destruction of Jerusalem. The 1000-year reign of Christ is currently happening in the hearts of believers. The only fulfillment left is for Jesus to return in judgement and begin God's heavenly kingdom.

2. **Premillenial** – A theory that predicts future fulfillment will begin with the Rapture, the Antichrist, Tribulation, a literal 1000-year reign of Jesus and then the final battle of Armageddon. Satan will finally be defeated and thrown into the Lake of Fire, along with all who follow him and are judged by God. Then God's heavenly kingdom will begin.

3. **Postmillenial** – A theory that depicts the 1000-year reign of Christ as the figurative time between his first coming and his second, in which the world will be "Christianized" and made a better place.

But no one knows the day or the hour of this happening,
not even the angels in Heaven, no, not even the Son—only the Father. Keep
your eyes open, keep on the alert, for you
do not know when the time will be.
Mark 13:32-33 (J. B. Phillips)

5

Grace vs. Works
Growing in the Light of Grace

And we, who with unveiled faces all reflect the Lord's glory, are being transformed into his likeness with ever-increasing glory, which comes from the Lord, who is the Spirit.
II Corinthians 3:18

In the tenth chapter of Luke's Gospel, an "expert in the law" asked Jesus, "What must I do to inherit eternal life?" The question of good works being necessary for salvation is one of the most controversial topics in Christianity. The Apostle Paul wrote, "For it is by grace you have been saved, through faith—and this not from yourselves, it is the gift of God—not by works, so that no one can boast" (Ephesians 2:8-10). He seems to indicate that there is nothing we can do in order to be saved and that salvation has already been given as a gift to those who believe.

However, Jesus gave the questioning man a much different answer; "What is written in the Law? How do you read it?" He answered: "'Love the Lord your God with all your heart and with all your soul and with all your strength and with all your mind'; and, 'Love your neighbor as yourself.'" "You have answered correctly," Jesus replied. "Do this and you will live." Does this appear to be a contradiction? Did Paul, writing years later, change the rules of salvation? Are Jesus and Paul in disagreement when it comes to salvation? Actually, the difference between Jesus' and Paul's lessons lies in the difference between sanctification and justification.

In their simplest definitions, the word sanctification means "to be set apart" and justification means "to be declared righteous in God's sight." In Luke's story, Jesus shows the expert in the law that, while he appears to be in a right relationship with God, it is required of God's people to be set apart and take care of one another. In the Ephesian's passage, Paul is clearly drawing a line in the sand. Paul tells his audience that there is nothing they can do to be justified in God's sight. Salvation is given freely, without cost, to those who believe. However, Paul does not let his audience off the hook. Paul continues his thought by saying yes, you are saved by grace, but you were sanctified (set apart), "…in Christ Jesus to do good works, which God prepared in advance for us to do."

What are these works which we were set apart to do? There are some works which should be commonly performed by all of God's children. I Peter 4:8-10, for example, directs us to "love each other deeply, because love covers over a multitude of sins." We are challenged to "offer hospitality to one another without grumbling." And we are told that we should "use whatever gift [we have] received to serve others, faithfully administering God's grace in its various forms." There are also some individual works, or works not intended for everyone, which we carry out as part of our personal duties. Peter continues in verse 11: "If anyone speaks, he should do it as one speaking the very words of God. If anyone serves, he should do it with the strength God provides, so that in all things God may be praised through Jesus Christ." Like Paul, Peter leaves no room for selfish pride when it comes to matters of justification or sanctification. Every good work we perform is done with the strength God provides so that God may be praised. When I first became a Christian, I think I might have fully understood what acts of service God had set me apart to perform. I served in the music ministry by storing, transporting, setting up, and tearing down all the sound equipment for our church. We had a kitchen and a space which groups would rent out for special events, and I would serve as a cook, a waiter, and even a janitor. I participated in Bible studies with other people who had the desire to come to faith in Jesus. If someone needed help to move, I was the first one there to help. If someone needed a ride, I would be one of the first people called. Many people called me the "most serving person" in our particular ministry. I truly believed I was selflessly doing God's will for God's glory, and most people would have agreed with me.

My holy aura lasted until new leaders were being chosen to shepherd our small groups and I was not among them. I was hurt. I felt I was unfairly overlooked and pointed out all the things I had been doing and how much I deserved to be considered a leader in our congregation. One night at a birthday party, I made my feelings known with not a little bitterness. One of my good friends approached me that night and asked me a life-changing question: "Why do you think God chose to save you?" I had to think about it. Did I honestly believe that God chose to grant me salvation so I could be glorified as a leader in my congregation? Was it not more likely that God had set me apart to do the work I had been doing to demonstrate the love of God to others through acts of service? After thirteen years of being a Christian, I still ask myself that same question when things do not seem to be going the way I feel they should go. Why did God choose to justify and sanctify me? To quote

Luke's expert in the law, I am convinced I was saved so that I may, "Love the Lord [my] God with all [my] heart and with all [my] soul and with all [my] strength and with all [my] mind"; and, "Love [my] neighbor as [myself]."

GRACE VS. WORKS:
Growing in the Light of Grace

Stuff to Talk Through With a Friend
* What is God's will for my life; what has God set me apart to do?
* Am I willing to let God's grace rule in my life or do I feel compelled to work for my salvation?
* Am I willing to trust that God's purpose for me will be revealed in God's timing?

Things to Do If You Want to Grow
* Choose an area you want to grow in and pick an activity that will stretch your faith in that area. When complete, go over the results with a friend and determine how much was done through your own effort, and how much was grace.
* Serve in an area you feel confident about, and then serve in an area you don't feel confident about. Discuss the results with a spiritual friend and note any growth in either/both cases.

References for Further Bible Study
Romans 3:23-26, 12:3 • Galatians 3:1-14 • Colossians 4:6 • Jeremiah 29:11 • Psalm 138:8

Additional Resources
Transforming Grace, Living Confidently in God's Unfailing Love by Jerry Bridges
In the Grip of Grace: Your Father Always Caught You. He Still Does by Max Lucado
Ragamuffin Gospel by Brennan Manning
Romans: The Heart Set Free by Gordon Ferguson
The Guilty Soul's Guide to Grace by Samuel Laing
Strong in the Grace by Thomas A. Jones
The Complete Guide to Grace by James L. Lefler

For additional resources or to join our online community, go to:
http://fieldguide.faith21.org

6

The Sovereignty of God
Who Is in Control Here?

> *"I make known the end from the beginning, from ancient times, what is still to come. I say: My purpose will stand, and I will do all that I please."*
> Isaiah 46:10

Control: ever since we were babies, we have striven for control. We wanted the control of our playmate's toy, control over what we wanted to wear at school, control over with whom and where we would spend our time. Finally, we realized that we weren't really in control of anything and pledged to let God take control. As the words of the wonderful hymn *When I Survey the Wondrous Cross*—"Love so amazing, so divine, demands my soul, my life, my all"—drifted through our minds, we knew that everything would be different and we would never be the same. However, as the days turned to weeks, we realized that some things had not changed. We still wanted to be in control.

I had been a Christian for over ten years, yet never truly understood who was in control until I had none. When I left the military, I joined a large consulting company, moved to another state and felt completely in control of my life; but things were not as they seemed. For over three years, I would leave before everyone in my house awoke, returning just in time to put my two young girls to bed. But I was in control. I traveled a hundred miles a day in heavy traffic and saw my family for less than one hour a day. But I was in control. My relationship with God and my family suffered. But I was in control—until that critical day when I wasn't. Unexpectedly laid off, unemployed with two small children, I finally began to understand who was in control—and it was not me.

You have no doubt heard the phrase, "Stop worrying, God is in control," many times in your life. Maybe it is easy to believe when things are going well, and annoying when things are difficult. God asks in Job 1:8, "Have you considered my servant Job?" Job lost everything in his life and had to endure "help" from his friends until he finally received a chance to confront God. God responded in a most peculiar way to Job. God said nothing about why things happened or even how. Instead he spoke of who God was, and by extension, who Job was in comparison. This is strange to our worldly way of thinking. God essentially answers Job's seemingly righteous complaint by stating, "I am in control." Job considers all this and says in response, "Surely I spoke about things I did not understand, things too wonderful for me to know" (Job 42:3). Job understood. God created the world with all of us in it, and he is in control.

God has always been in control, but he does something incredible—he gives us a choice. We can obey or rebel, follow or try to lead, but no matter what the choice is, God is still in control. Queen Esther had a choice: try to save the Jewish people and risk her life, or do nothing. Her uncle Mordecai told her, "Don't think that you will escape the fate of all the Jews because you are in the king's palace. If you keep silent at this time, liberation and deliverance will come to the Jewish people from another place, but you and your father's house will be destroyed. Who knows, perhaps you have come to the kingdom for such a time as this" (Esther 4:13-14).

Shadrach, Meshach and Abednego understood who was in control. Standing up for God, they were about to pay the ultimate price. They had a choice—give in and worship the statue, or refuse and die. Their response was, "Nebuchadnezzar, we don't need to give you an answer to this question. If the God we serve exists, then he can rescue us from the furnace of blazing fire, and he can rescue us from the power of you, the king. But even if he does not rescue us, we want you as king to know that we will not serve your gods or worship the gold statue you set up" (Daniel 3:16-18). They understood they had a choice, but God was in control. Standing up for the hard choice was not easy, but it was right.

Unfortunately, many times we try to do things ourselves without consulting God. It's at times like these that God reveals who is in control. "Do not be deceived: God cannot be mocked. A man reaps what he sows" (Galatians 6:7). I Samuel 4 tells the story of the Israelites meeting with defeat from the Philistines. After this setback, they decide what they need to do is carry the Ark of the Covenant with them into battle. They trust in an object, in their own strength, instead of God. The result did not bring glory to God. "So the Philistines fought, and Israel was defeated, and each man fled to his tent. The slaughter was severe—30,000 of the Israelite foot soldiers fell. The ark of God was captured, and Eli's two sons, Hophni and Phinehas, died" (I Samuel 4:10-11). There are times in our lives where we will try and do things ourselves, to "prove" that we are in control, and fail. The good news—God can still use these times for his plans. The rest of this story includes the death of the high priest Eli on hearing the news and the ascension of Samuel the prophet. God is in control.

When good or bad things happen, what should be our response?

* **Praise and Worship of God**
  "The LORD gave and the LORD has taken away; may the name of the LORD be praised" (Job 1:21). Everything we have is from God and is a gift.

* **Thanksgiving**
  "Giving thanks to God the Father for everything" (Ephesians 5:20).

* **Trust**
  "Trust in the Lord with all your heart; do not depend on your own understanding. Seek his will in all you do, and he will direct your paths" (Proverbs 3:5-6).

Remember, God does not promise an easy journey. Understanding God is in control means understanding we are not. God gives us a choice, but ultimately he is in control.

THE SOVEREIGNTY OF GOD: Who Is in Control Here?

Stuff to Talk Through With a Friend
* When am I most likely to try and take control of my life?
* In what areas of my life do I need to trust God more?
* Is my reaction the same during good times and bad?

Things to Do If You Want to Grow
* Encourage a brother or sister who is going through a hard time. Listen to them, and if they are open to it, share with them what you have learned.
* Take a day to pray to God about placing your trust in him.

References for Further Bible Study
* II Samuel 11—The life of Uriah the Hittite
* II Samuel 6—David tries to move the ark
* Genesis 27—Isaac and Jacob—Did Isaac really need to deceive Jacob?
* Jesus and the Cross
* Paul in prison

Additional Resources
The Unveiling: Exploring the Nature of God by Curt Simmons
The Victory of Surrender by Gordon Ferguson
More on the subject at www.CCEL.org

For additional resources or to join our online community, go to:
http://fieldguide.faith21.org

7

Who Is Saved?
Salvation Yesterday, Today and Tomorrow

Nevertheless, more and more men and women believed in the Lord and were added to their number.
Acts 5:14

If you are reading this, chances are you have recently made the most important decision of your life; you have decided to become a disciple of Jesus! The purpose of this chapter is to help increase your understanding; to help you see what being "saved" is really all about.

To get started, we must clear up a few things. First, let's talk about salvation in terms of the past. As you now believe, Jesus Christ came to the earth and died on the cross in order to save the world (John 3:16-17). In a general sense, his sacrifice on the cross for our salvation applies to everyone on the planet. John 1:9 says that Jesus "gives light to every man" with his coming. Now, does this mean that every person on earth is automatically saved simply because Jesus came? No (John 1:12). What it does mean is that, long before we were born or even aware of our need, the opportunity to be saved was made available to us through Jesus' sacrifice on the cross. The key for us is this: we must "receive him" (John 1:12) if his sacrifice is going to have any value for us.

So, what does "receive Jesus" mean for us today? Acts 2:36-39 shows us how to receive him. After hearing the message of the Cross, the people were very much affected by it (Acts 2:37). They not only believed what they heard, but they were personally "cut to the heart," so much so that they asked the apostles, "what shall we do?" Peter's response was, "Repent and be baptized…for the forgiveness of your sins. And you will receive the gift of the Holy Spirit" (Acts 2:38). This biblical example for salvation is still valid today, if a person is truly repentant and believing in Christ.

We learn from this passage that repentance and baptism are inseparable. It is at baptism that a person is initially saved from sin and "receives" the Holy Spirit. God's power works in conjunction with our repentant hearts to bring about this miracle. That is God's present-day plan for salvation as we understand it. Summarized in a few words: believe, repent and be baptized.

So, does salvation end with baptism? No, our responsibility to change doesn't stop after baptism. Yes, it is true that a conversion following the outline in Acts 2 is God's plan for salvation in that it is the initial point when we are saved and forgiven for our sins, but there is more to it than that. You see, God wants the same heart we had at baptism to be what we strive to maintain for the rest of our lives—a continual life of repentance. To accomplish this nearly impossible task, God gives us, at our conversion, his Holy Spirit as a deposit (II Corinthians 1:21-22) to assist and constantly renew us. The Holy Spirit is like a divine power source, giving us the supernatural ability to accomplish what we never could before on our own. Not just at-the-surface, superficial changes, mind you, but deep character changes in the areas of our lives where sin previously dominated.

The Bible often speaks of salvation in the present tense (Mathew 28:19-20; I John 5:2-4; Philippians 2:12-13). We see in these passages that our salvation, in the present tense, has everything to do with our decision to persevere in obedience. Obviously, it can never be achieved on our own talent, goodness or merit, but we still need to wholeheartedly go after it.

We can fail each other when conveying God's plan for salvation in two ways. The first would be to inadequately preach grace and put the burden completely on the person to be "good enough" to earn their way to Heaven. None of us are good enough, despite our best effort (Galatians 3:3), and therefore our only hope is to rely on the power of God's Holy Spirit. The second way we can fail to convey true salvation is to minimize God's expectation of continual, life-long growth and repentance after baptism—to preach "cheap grace." We see throughout scripture that God's expectation of obedience is very clear. What is even more amazing is to see the assurance following the expectation—that God will be there to help us fight the battle and to overcome (Philippians 1:6; II Peter 1:3).

God's expectation is not unreasonable, especially when we realize that it is God who is actually doing the work. The Holy Spirit continues to mold and shape us into the image of Jesus, as we strive to change. For us, it is supposed to be like two sides of one coin; the more we surrender to the Spirit in our hearts, the more capable we become in our obedience. The more obedient we are in our actions, the more surrendered we become to the Spirit (John 8:31-32). The Spirit of Christ *is* doing the work, but our willingness to surrender is what unleashes his power. This is why confessing our sins and being open about our weaknesses is so important. As we live a repentant, obedient and transparent life before God, our salvation is continually renewed. The blood of Jesus continually cleanses us of our sins (I John 1:7).

The Bible says that the ultimate goal of our faith is the salvation of our souls (I Peter 1:9). When we think about salvation in the future tense, we realize that we persevere not only to be freed from our sins today, but to keep our hearts pure in order to make it to Heaven (Hebrews 3:14; Revelation 2:7, 2:11, 2:17). As long as we persevere until the end and do not turn away from him, we will get to spend eternity with God in Heaven. What an amazing thought!

"Who is saved?" someone might ask. When we get down to it, God's plan of salvation for us is to: 1) hear the message of the Cross; 2) believe it; 3) repent of sins; 4) be baptized; and 5) persevere until the end. Jesus died to save us from our sins, not merely the penalty of our sins (Mathew 1:21). This means that we should fully expect to live changed lives and never lose heart, remembering that we have everything we need to be disciples of Jesus (II Peter 1:3-9).

WHO IS SAVED:
Salvation Yesterday, Today and Tomorrow

Stuff to Talk Through With a Friend

* The "sinner's prayer" is a man-made concept that claims a person is saved when he "prays Jesus into his heart." Many who subscribe to this teaching believe that baptism isn't necessary for salvation. They think it is an outward sign of an inward reality. How does the biblical teaching in Acts 2 differ? What does a person receive at baptism (Acts 2:38) that makes the "sinners prayer" way to salvation incomplete?

* The doctrine of "once saved always saved" teaches that once a person becomes a Christian they can never lose their relationship with God. What does Hebrews 10:26 say about that? Why do you think the "once saved always saved" concept is appealing to some even though it isn't accurate?

* What do you need to repent of today? Is a life of repentance (constant heart change) something you are willing to strive for, throughout the rest of your life?

Things to Do If You Want to Grow

* In what ways might you struggle with compromising the true biblical doctrine of salvation?
* What had you believed about being "saved" before becoming a disciple?
* How do you feel about scriptures like Ephesians 4:1-6 and 1 Peter 3:18-22?

References for Further Bible Study
Mark 16:16 • 1 John 1:5-10

Additional Resources
Who Is My Brother? by F. LaGard Smith
Will the Real Heretics Please Stand Up: A New Look at Today's Evangelical Church in the Light of Early Christianity by David W. Bercot
Baptism: the Water that Divides DVD by Douglas Jacoby

For additional resources or to join our online community, go to:
http://fieldguide.faith21.org

CHRISTIAN CONUNDRUMS
Hell

The Bible very clearly warns us about Hell. It is described in vivid detail as a real place of scorching fire and hideous torment. However, one very important fact about Hell is not stated in absolute terms: the duration. How long will those without Christ suffer in Hell?

Over the centuries, several ideas have sprung forth within Christianity (some with more scriptural backing than others):

Eternal Hell

The Bible indicates that the fires of Hell will burn for all eternity. The belief is that unrepentant sinners will suffer in Hell forever, with no hope of dying or being saved. God made man an eternal soul with the power to decide where he or she will spend eternity. The consequences of that choice are forever.

Terminal Hell

The Bible speaks of the finality of the punishment for those without Christ. The belief is that sinners will suffer in Hell in accordance to what they have done, and no more. Once the full measure of their punishment has been suffered, they will be destroyed. Eternal life is a gift only for Christians.

Temporary Hell

The Bible says that, in the end, every person will confess Jesus as Lord. The belief is that everyone who is not a Christian will go to Hell and stay there, suffering horribly until they repent and have paid for all the wrong they have done. Then all will be saved and go to Heaven.

And these will go off to eternal punishment, but the true men to eternal life.
Matthew 25:46 (J.B. Phillips)

8

Hell

Abandon All Hope, You Who Enter Here

> *"Then they will go away to eternal punishment,*
> *but the righteous to eternal life."*
> Matthew 25:46

All things have their antitheses, from personalities to foods to colors. However, where the idea of Heaven is generally embraced, many remain skittish, resistant or even downright offended by the notion of an actual Hell. Many prefer to dismiss this emotionally-loaded truth rather than accept it and consider the consequences. Hell is jolting and inconvenient, opposing an immature view of God. "How could a loving God send people to Hell?" we cry. Like the Bereans in Acts 17, we can find answers by examining the scriptures for ourselves.

A saga of epic proportions burst onto the spiritual arena in 1984. *Scientific American*, an intellectual brief, published the account of a drilling experiment conducted in Siberia by a team of Russian scientists. After boring into the Earth approximately nine miles deep, they discovered a cavity with temperatures reaching 180 degrees. Their exploit circulated the globe rapidly, acquiring outrageous embellishments along the way, including a temperature increase to 2000 degrees and microphones capturing the gut-wrenching screams of the damned. The world was abuzz with the idea that these scientists had broken through to Hell. This legend, known as the "Well to Hell," persists to this day. In 1991, American cardiologist Dr. Maurice S. Rawlings authored the best-selling *Beyond Death's Door*, recounting the posthumous experiences of multiple patients who were revived after being declared clinically dead. Instead of the beckoning, brightly-lit tunnel common to cinematic features, patients relayed being thrust into extreme heat amongst screaming inhabitants in a dark, subterranean place. These accounts are dubious at best, but do carry three consistent, biblical teachings:

* Hell is real (Matthew 10:28; Luke 12:5)
* It is the destiny of the lost (Psalms 9:17; Matthew 11:23)
* You just do not want to go there (Luke 16:27; Hebrews 10:26-27)

Immortality is a natural longing, for it is of supernatural design (Ecclesiastes 3:11). The human pursuit of longevity has been manifested in many forms: non-essential cosmetic surgeries, lying about one's age, a plethora of diets and even extremes like body freezing (cryogenics). Unfortunately, we can fool our minds and mirrors, but not our DNA! Our best efforts are ultimately futile; eternal life comes only through Jesus Christ (II Timothy 1:10). We are innately aware that physical death is not the final curtain on our lives. Even most eulogies assume the deceased is in Heaven or "a better place," regardless of their spiritual condition. This poetic reasoning may comfort the bereaved, but it is inaccurate. The reality is that Heaven is unsentimentally reserved for the redeemed

(Matthew 7:21). Unfortunately, that number will probably be nominal (Matthew 7:13-14). Therefore, post-mortem, the great mass of humanity will be spending the rest of their time *somewhere else* with *somebody else* (Matthew 25:41). On the contrary, the dead outside of Christ are not "in a better place" (Isaiah 14:9-11).

The reality of Hell rests on the Bible's own credibility. The Bible describes itself in no uncertain terms: flawless, pure, proclaiming *every* word to be God's very own (Psalm 18:30; II Timothy 3:16-17; I Thessalonians 2:13). It doesn't make it easy to believe; scripture is full of mind-boggling, unprovable tales: a woman turned into salt (Genesis 19:26), a talking donkey (Numbers 22:21-33), water turned into premium wine (John 2:1-11), and more. The Bible also asks us to trust that Jesus, a poor carpenter who called himself God (John 8:58), is the only completely sane and rational man who ever lived. Second only to this truth, the Bible's greatest claim is the existence of Hell. These absolutes require humble acceptance or total rejection; there is no middle ground (Proverbs 30:5-6).

The Old Testament, largely written in Hebrew, often spoke of *sheol*. This was the abode of the dead, both the righteous (Genesis 37:34-35), and the wicked (Isaiah 14:9-11). When Hellenistic Jews translated the Old Testament into Greek (the *Septuagint*), Sheol was usually rendered the grave (Psalm 6:5), the pit (Proverbs 1:12), or death (Job 17:16). Greek Jews also translated Sheol as Hades, a term used in Greek mythology for a gloomy underworld of departed spirits.

Jesus spoke of vivid afterlife distinctions in Luke 16:19-31 (the rich man and Lazarus) and Luke 23:39-43 (the crucified thieves). These passages shed more light on an interim place after death, where judgment is awaited in *separate* areas. The saved rest in bliss (Paradise, "Abraham's bosom"), while the lost wrestle in anguish. The Greek New Testament also contains the words Gehenna and Tartarus, designating a harsh place of *final* punishment, which is often translated for us as Hell, as opposed to Hades, the interim place. As if all these terms were not confusing enough, some Bible translations use Hades and Hell interchangeably and others omit Hades entirely and only say Hell.

Jesus spoke about Hell more than anyone else in the Bible. He prefaced many of these powerful and graphic pronouncements with "I tell you the truth." Consider these harrowing descriptions:

* Agonizing heat (Luke 16:24)
* Banishment from God (Mathew 7:23; II Thessalonians 1:8-10)
* Everlasting worms (Isaiah 66:24)
* Eternal fire (Matthew 18:8; Mark 9:43)
* Excruciating pain (Mark 9:49)
* Final punishment (Daniel 12:1-2; Matthew 25:46; II Peter 2:4-10)
* No way out (Luke 16:26)
* Smoky (Revelation 14:11)
* Totally dark (II Peter 2:17; Jude 13)
* Unquenchable thirst (Luke 16:24)

The Bible teaches a physical death phenomenon understood only by God. In Hell, you're still you (Matthew 5:22-30; Luke 16:23-31), fully conscious, faculties alert and in *torment*. Repentance will come too late. There is neither escape nor reprieve, at least until all has been paid. Hell is not the denouement of a fair-weather god. Rather, as free-will creations, we decide our own destination (Deuteronomy 30:11-20). God is unwilling to be eternally separated from anyone (II Peter 3:9), but he honors our choice, whether it brings him happiness or heartbreak. As C.S. Lewis said, in the end either we will say to God "thy will be done" or he will say to us "thy will be done."

These truths can bring us heartbreak, but they are not something for us to fear. In Matthew 12:40, Jesus remarkably promises to spend three days and nights in the heart of the earth, proclaiming victory over Hades (Matthew 16:18). Peter, recalling David's words in Psalm 16:10, preaches about this in Acts 2:31, and Paul echoes the thought in Ephesians 4:9. Jesus, our champion, has defeated the power of Hell and offers us life eternal with him. May we do all we can to live lives worthy of Heaven, and seek with all our might to save others from the fire.

HELL: Abandon All Hope, You Who Enter Here

Stuff to Talk Through With a Friend
* What have I believed about Hell and why?
* Do my beliefs match or contradict the Bible's teaching on Hell?
* Have I had any unbiblical thinking about Hell? If so, what kind?
* How would I explain Hell to someone who asks?
* Do I believe I know anyone on his way to Hell because of his lifestyle? If so, does Jude 23 prompt me to help? If not, why?

Things to Do If You Want to Grow
* Study what the Bible says about Hell and be absolutely clear about what you believe.
* Prepare yourself to handle this difficult topic with outsiders.
* Make a list of ways to help move 5 new people towards Christ. Pray, and go DO it!

References for Further Bible Study
Deuteronomy 32:22 • Psalm 49:14-15, 139:8, 141:7 • Proverbs 9:18, 15:24
Ecclesiastes 9:10 • Ezekiel 31:16, 32:29-30 • Hosea 13:14

Additional Resources
23 Minutes in Hell by Bill Wiese
The Prospect of Immortality by Robert C.W. Ettinger
Heaven & Hell: Terminal Punishment online paper by Douglas Jacoby

For additional resources or to join our online community, go to:
http://fieldguide.faith21.org

9

Heaven
Great Expectations

"Do not let your hearts be troubled. Trust in God; trust also in me. In my Father's house are many rooms. If it were not so, I would have told you. I am going there to prepare a place for you. And if I go and prepare a place for you, I will come back and take you to be with me so that you also may be where I am."
John 14:1-4

One of the most inspiring and yet mysterious concepts in our Christian journey is that of Heaven, our final destination. Often portrayed in popular culture with fluffy clouds and angels playing harps, we can easily forget what God has told us about that very real place. The Bible teaches that Heaven is not just a lofty idea but a promise, a return on an investment, and a fulfillment for those who dedicate their lives to God.

The first thing we must consider is that the Bible draws a clear correlation between our earthly lives and Heaven. Romans 2:6 states, "God will give to each person according to what he has done. To those who by persistence in doing good seek glory, honor and immortality, he will give eternal life." We know that God doesn't make promises lightly, and we can trust that his word is accurate and true (Numbers 23:19). It is important to remember that our salvation into Heaven is based on God's choice to reward us for the actions we have taken from a heart prompted by the Spirit to do good in this life (Matthew 25:31-6). In fact, good actions in our mortal life should be thought of as a compounding investment, earning us the reward many times over in Heaven. What an amazing deal! Not only have we been forgiven of our sins, but now God is giving us a reward for helping others. This reward is above and beyond what is already promised us in this life when we love each other (Proverbs 11:25)!

In case you haven't noticed, the world does not have the same priorities as God. As Christians living in this world, we must keep a constant guard against all the things that jeopardize our relationship with God (I John 2:15). Living a constant guard doesn't seem like a lot of fun, but then again, life in this world is not meant to be easy. In fact, Jesus warns us that we will have troubles (John 16:33), and these troubles are part of God's refining process that will achieve our goal of reaching Heaven (II Corinthians 4:17).

The prospect of Heaven is an amazing gift not just to be enjoyed once we get there, but also a gift we can take advantage of today. Jesus is offering us freedom from the troubles of this world by trusting in him and by longing for the place he is preparing for us (John 14:1-4). However, while living in joyful expectation of Heaven sounds like a welcome relief from the pressures of life, it does not come easy or without practice. Thankfully, life offers plenty of opportunities to apply our belief in God's promise of a better afterlife.

In my experience, I have never found a better time to hone this skill of trusting in God than during long periods of financial pressure. As I write this, I have yet to find another job after having been laid off nearly a year ago. Unemployment can be spiritually debilitating, and the stories of those who have chosen suicide or murder when faced with financial difficulties illustrate how extreme these situations can become. Choosing to invest my time in service to God and bringing others to know him has been a welcome outlet for me. I try to think of myself like Paul. He was locked in prison on several occasions throughout his life, but chose to use this time to write letters of encouragement to the churches. Though my sufferings during my time in this financial prison cannot compare to what Paul went through, I have decided to focus my mind and heart, not on worrying, but on the things that matter eternally (Matthew 6:33-34).

Jesus tells us in Matthew 6:19, "Do not store up for yourselves treasures on earth, where moth and rust destroy, and where thieves break in and steal. But store up for yourselves treasures in Heaven, where moth and rust do not destroy, and where thieves do not break in and steal. For where your treasure is, there your heart will be also." You might think this scripture could be more easily applied when you don't have many treasures to store up. Unfortunately, lack of material treasure can bring about more of a longing to attain it than if you were already financially stable. Why do you think the disciples were so surprised when Jesus told them it was hard for a rich man to enter the Kingdom of God? It wasn't because they were rich; it was because they wanted to be rich (Mark 10:24-26)! I have experienced *both* sides. In my current state of financial strain, I am faced every day with the task of accepting where God is taking me and being content along the journey (Philippians 4:11-12). Focusing my efforts on things that will build God's kingdom and spending extra time with others in need has been the best distraction from self-pity or despair that I have found.

Putting God first in our lives, especially when times are hard, is only possible if we first make the decision to steer our minds into the direction of eternal priorities (Colossians 3:1-4). Whatever stress we face, we must not forget the glory that awaits us. Of all the scriptures regarding Heaven, none make the point quite like this one: "And I heard a loud voice from the throne saying, now the dwelling of God is with men, and he will live with them. They will be his people, and God himself will be with them and be their God. He will wipe every tear from their eyes. There will be no more death or mourning or crying or pain, for the old order of things has passed away" (Revelation 21:3). Heaven is the greatest goal we can aim for in our lives. Nothing compares to it. Money and pleasures can come and go, but the promise for Christians of a heavenly home needs to be what we most desire (Philippians 3:20-21).

HEAVEN: Great Expectations

Stuff to Talk Through With a Friend
* How does knowing that life's problems are part of God's plan to better you change your outlook on life?
* What can you do to put heavenly priorities first every day?
* How have your views of Heaven changed since becoming a Christian?
* How does your knowledge of Heaven help you with issues of stress or worry?

Things to Do If You Want to Grow
* Look for ways to contribute to the Kingdom of Heaven with your unique skills and talents.
* Make it a point to let heavenly priorities guide your daily schedule of events.
* When asked for help, consider it an opportunity to store treasures in Heaven and seize the day!

References for Further Bible Study
Isaiah 65:17-25 • Hebrews 11:16 • II Peter 3:10-13 • Revelation 21-22

Additional Resources
Heaven by Randy Alcorn
Driven by Eternity: Making Your Life Count Today & Forever by John Bevere
A Travel Guide to Heaven by Anthony DeStefano
What Happens After We Die? by Douglas Jacoby

For additional resources or to join our online community, go to:
http://fieldguide.faith21.org

Section Two
Discipleship: Becoming Like Jesus

A divine conspiracy is set against us. God will bring anything and everything into our lives in order to help us to become more like his Son. There will be trials, persecutions and hardships, as well as joys, peace and times of rest. The next twenty-one chapters will help us deal with the choices that come our way as we learn the lessons God has planned for us.

> *Moreover, we know that to those who love God, who are called according to his plan, everything that happens fits into a pattern for good. For God, in his foreknowledge, shoes them to bear the family likeness of his Son, that he might be the eldest of a family of many brothers.*
>
> Romans 8:28-29 (J.B. Phillips)

10

Prayer
Can We Talk?

> ...*pray all the time*
> I Thessalonians 5:17 (The Message)

The Bible is filled with countless examples of people communicating with God. While the biblical lessons on prayer could take a lifetime to learn, our connection with God simply starts with opening our mouths.

In the beginning, God created Adam and Eve and had a perfect relationship with them. Then they sinned and everything changed. The Bible teaches that they heard God in the cool of the day and hid from him to avoid the consequences of their sin (Genesis 3:8-9). The first couple on Earth had the opportunity to speak directly with God to ask for forgiveness for their sins, yet they chose to hide out of fear and shame.

Disconnection from God is Satan's greatest scheme. He does not want us to talk with God. He wants us to run and hide. He hates for us to have a loving relationship with our Father. His goal is to tear us apart. He does this by leading us into sin, which separates us from God (Isaiah 59:1-2). The only way back is to repent and confess our sin. Thankfully, God longs to forgive us and restore our relationship to him (I Peter 5:10-11).

One of my favorite things to do is to walk in "the cool of the day." I ask God to walk with me and choose to be vulnerable with him so we can talk freely. This is a great time to talk about anything that is on my mind. Sometimes, I just listen and admire his amazing creation. These are priceless moments. As God looked for Adam and Eve in the garden, I believe he looks to have a connection with us every day.

We can learn about how *not* to have a relationship with God through the story of Cain, Adam and Eve's first son. Cain became jealous of Abel, his brother, and even though God encouraged Cain to repent of his sinful attitude (Genesis 4:7), he sinned even more by killing his brother and then lying about it. God had to confront him because there were consequences to his sin. God lovingly warns those he loves. Today, he often speaks to us and guides us through his Word (II Timothy 4:16-17). It is our choice as to whether or not we are going to listen. We can learn from Cain's bad decision and choose to wisely listen when God speaks to us. Just as Cain's relationship with God was severed by his own choice (Genesis 4:16), our shame may often lead us to cut off intimate conversations with God.

Abraham is a great example of prayer. In Genesis 18:16-33, we see how Abraham pleaded for Sodom and Gomorrah. God listened and talked with him as a friend. After much haggling, God agreed to not destroy Sodom if there were only ten righteous men living there, instead of 50 men as originally agreed. This is an unbelievable moment of great courage on Abraham's part, which should remind us to have faith to pray for all people, no matter how challenging the situation. We have the opportunity to plead with God for the salvation of our friends and family. Take heart, he is listening.

In Genesis 25:19-24, while Rebekah was pregnant, we can imagine her wonder and maybe her pain at the same time. It is hard to imagine what it would feel like to be pregnant with twins who were prophesied to become a people of great strife. Instead of complaining or doubting God's great plan, we learn that she simply inquired of the Lord (vv 22-23) and he answered her. Rebekah dared to ask what many of us want to, "Why?" God knows the answer and whether it is for our benefit to know or not. Either way, it is okay to respectfully ask.

Sometimes we may have to wrestle with God for a blessing as Jacob did (Genesis 32:22-32), though we need to be ready for the pain that might bring. There was a time in my life when all I wanted was a child. I miscarried twice and had difficulty conceiving. It was a time full of heartache, but I never stopped praying and reading God's word. Each day, I had to choose to believe and trust God's word with all my heart. It took faith and tons of support from my friends and family. Ultimately, what brought me through was prayer. God has blessed me with a child. The greater blessing is a deep intimacy with him that I only learned through pain.

From the beginning of time, we can see God's passion for communion with us. Hebrews 11, the great Hall of Faith, shows us ordinary men and women having an incredible relationship with God. Every single one of them struggled, yet they leave us with an example of a faithful relationship to God. They also point to the One who can bring back the original plan of fellowship with our Father (Hebrews 12:1-3). Jesus' submission and respect toward God is the perfect example of how we are to interact with both our earthly and heavenly fathers. The twelve apostles clearly learned this lesson from him. They were with Jesus when he prayed and saw him get up at daybreak (Luke 5:16), withdraw often (Luke 4:42) and spend the night praying (Luke 6:12). They saw that his relationship with God was unique. The apostles humbly asked to be taught to pray, and Jesus showed them (Luke 11:1-11).

Jesus didn't stop with just teaching us to pray. He left us the Holy Spirit, an amazing gift (John 14:15-25). The Spirit is another way that God speaks to us. He will counsel and teach us, remind us of the truth and always be with us. As Christians, that voice in our hearts that guides us is more than just our conscience. It's God's Holy Spirit! We must listen to him and not grieve him (Ephesians 4:30).

I recently was at home and something nudged me to go to a nearby coffee house. As I walked and prayed, I ran into an old friend who had also recently become a mom. I was able to share my faith with her and plant some seeds. I realized afterwards that it was the Spirit nudging me to do something as mundane, or so I thought, as getting some coffee. I planted seeds along the way, "walked with God in the cool of the day," and he encouraged me with a tall, soy, vanilla latte. A conversation with God started for me, as it can for you, by simply opening my mouth and praying to him.

PRAYER: Can We Talk?

Stuff to Talk Through With a Friend
* Are there any hidden sins that are hindering your conversations with God?
* What is God trying to show you through his word?
* Who in your life needs prayer?
* Is there a struggle in your life that God is using to build intimacy with him?
* How can you imitate Jesus' relationship with God?
* How is the Spirit nudging you?

Things to Do If You Want to Grow
* Confess anything that is separating you from God.
* Make a list of all your family, friends and enemies and pray for them daily for 21 days.
* Choose one day a week that you will walk with God "in the cool of the day."
* Journal about your most recent Spirit-led moment.

References for Further Bible Study
Mark 14:35-36 • Romans 8 • Colossians 1:9-14 • 1 Timothy 2:8 • Hebrews 4:16 • James 4:2-3, 5:15 • 1 John 5:14-15

Additional Resources
The Complete E.M. Bounds on Prayer
The Four Streams: How Christ Heals our Hearts by John Eldredge—Disk One
Walking with God by John Eldredge
Be Still My Soul by Samuel Laing

For additional resources or to join our online community, go to:
http://fieldguide.faith21.org

11

MMM...God's Word!
Our Daily Bread

> *All Scripture is God-breathed and is useful for teaching, rebuking, correcting and training in righteousness, so that the man of God may be thoroughly equipped for every good work.*
> **II Timothy 3:16-17**

Whether physical or spiritual, food is essential to our daily lives. In fact, our consumption of God's word is more than a gift, it is a spiritual necessity. In Matthew 4, we learn that the very Word of God is what our daily spiritual diet must consist of. We need to be feeding ourselves spiritually to truly live spiritual lives. In today's world, we have the Bible on the Internet, on our phones and MP3 players—just a click away. The Word of God is readily available to us. This chapter will give some practical tools to help our relationship with God grow as we seek him daily. Remember, one does not grow without food. Bon appetite!

The Bible reveals five major food groups which feed our spiritual lives: 1) reading God's Word, 2) committing it to memory, 3) meditating on it, 4) prayer and 5) fellowship with other Christians. These five things should be our daily regiment. They are spiritual acts of worship that should be prompted by our love for God. When we apply them to our lives daily, it is like having our own spiritual I.V., constantly feeding us.

Early in my Christian walk, people would spend time with me praying and reading God's word, or suggesting scripture for me to read on my own. This was instrumental in helping me develop a strong foundation of spending time with God on a daily basis. When I first started reading God's word, I didn't want to put it down for hours. If this is something you are doing, then praise God! Yet, a more focused reading has many benefits as well. I soon learned to read only one chapter a day, in order to absorb more of what I was reading. For some of us, reading can be a daunting task, and simplifying our time with God doesn't allow Satan to overwhelm us.

The more we seek God through his Word and apply it to our daily lives, the more righteously equipped we become. The more we live what we learn, the more we will be men and women of God who choose to walk in his character, and not our own. Do not forget that we also need his protection; we need his armor, for we are not without an enemy (Ephesians 6:10-17).

In addition to reading the scriptures, we need to commit them to memory. How was Jesus able to recite the scriptures, as he did throughout the gospels? Was Jesus carrying around all the scrolls of the Old Testament? No, but he did have them in his heart and mind (Proverbs 3:1). Memorizing God's word is his desire for us as well. Having it in our hearts and minds will help us apply it to our lives. The convenient access to his Word through today's technology is great, but the goal is for us to be living his Word, not just be able to quickly find a passage. The idea of memorizing scripture can be a daunting thought, so here are some tips to get started: highlight or underline scriptures that stand out to you as you read. Write them out on paper and then close your eyes and imagine each word. Recite them to yourself, or even out loud, throughout your day. If you are like me, singing them to your own melody will help a lot, and be very enjoyable.

Matthew gives us an example of why it is so important to memorize scripture. When Jesus is being tempted by Satan, he is able to defend himself by quoting scriptures from memory (Matthew 4:1-4; Deuteronomy 8:3). In the same way, whenever we are tempted, challenged in our faith, persecuted, whenever we are sad and mourning, feeling hopeless and depressed, we can have the Word of God engraved into our hearts and minds. This will strengthen, encourage and comfort us, and help us to do the same for others. As an added bonus, when we are asked to give an answer for why we believe, we will always be equipped (II Corinthians 3:3).

Memorization of scripture goes hand in hand with meditation on it. To meditate means to reflect upon, ponder or contemplate in the mind. It is simply the focus of one's mind on God's word. What are our minds usually focused on: our kids, school, work, money, traffic, sports, food, clothes, TV? Are they consumed with our "To Do" lists? Continuing to feed ourselves spiritually throughout the day is not always easy; things need to get done, and our minds will always have thoughts about everything this life holds. However, bringing God into our thoughts helps to protect us from being consumed by the fruitlessness of our earthly cares and desires (Colossians 3:1-2).

Setting our minds and hearts on Christ Jesus and his Word is true meditation. It can be done all day long, no matter where you are or what you're doing. Are you stressed out, worried about your job, is money tight, are you frustrated and impatient while stuck in traffic, are you being challenged and tempted? Take a deep breath and think of Jesus, think of his words, meditate on his character and his attitude. Focus your mind on God and his promises. Set your mind on heaven, not on the things of this world.

The other two components of a healthy spiritual diet are prayer and fellowship with other Christians. Prayer is an essential part of our spiritual lives because we are directly communicating with God and focusing our thoughts on him (Philippians 4:8-9). Fellowship is communion with God and our fellow believers. The Greek word for it is "koinonia." Its general meaning is community, communion, joint participation, sharing and intimacy (Acts 2:42-46). These topics both have separate chapters dedicated to them.

MMM... GOD'S WORD!:
Our Daily Bread

Stuff to Talk Through With a Friend
* How would you respond to someone who told you that the Bible is just a book of philosophy?
* How are reading the Bible and praying connected to each other? Can you make it with one and not the other? Why or why not?

Things to Do If You Want to Grow
* Read a selection of your favorite passages from a different translation of the Bible. How does the verse hit you differently, or the same, in the different version?
* Read a book of the Bible that seems to have no relevance in your life right now (for example, one of the minor Old Testament prophets) and record the lessons it teaches you.
* Read one of the Psalms aloud as a prayer to God. Incorporate the same language from the psalm into your own original prayer.

References for Further Bible Study
* Reading the Bible: Psalm 119; Proverbs 1-4
* Memorization: Matthew 4:1-4
* Meditation: Joshua 1:8
* Prayer: I Thessalonians 5:16-18; Mark 1:35; Luke 5:16; John 16:33; Hebrews 5:7
* Fellowship: II Corinthians 13:14; I Thessalonians 5:11; Romans 12:9-16

Additional Resources
Rick Warren's Bible Study Methods by Rick Warren
Getting the Most from the Bible by G. Steve Kinnard
How to Read the Bible for All Its Worth by Gordon Fee and Douglas Stuart
How We Got the Bible by Douglas Jacoby
How We Got the Bible and Why You Can Trust It by Mike Taliaferro

For additional resources or to join our online community, go to:
http://fieldguide.faith21.org

12

Let It Go
What Should I Leave Behind?

You were taught, with regard to your former way of life, to put off your old self, which is being corrupted by its deceitful desires; to be made new in the attitude of your minds; and to put on the new self, created to be like God in true righteousness and holiness.
Ephesians 4:22-24

Boxes, boxes, boxes. Every time I move there are more boxes. Things to give away, things to throw away, to pack carefully and mark fragile or to cram in. I've made international moves to Brazil, Russia, Ukraine and the US, and it is amazing how after getting rid of everything I don't need, and bringing only what I can fit in suitcases, I can acquire so much stuff in a year.

The same thing happens to me spiritually. I pick up many habits: from how I dress, walk and talk, to what I read and whom I hang out with. Some bring me closer to God; others make me blend in more with the world around me. When I became a Christian, I realized that in order to make it to my ultimate destination, I needed to pack up my old life and leave it behind (Luke 14:33). I was in college at the time, living with two guys, which I thought was fine because they were like brothers to me. However, as I studied the Bible, I learned that everything is permissible, but not everything is beneficial (I Corinthians 10:23). I knew that if I wanted to change my life, I needed to move out. Not wanting to offend my friends, I prayed hard about the talk I needed to have with those guys and sought advice about what to say and how to say it with love and respect. After explaining the reason for the changes they had been seeing in me, I told them I wanted to move out. They were very supportive, but asked, "Was it something we did?" To which I responded, "No, it's something I have to do." I was able to leave behind the lifestyle I had with them, yet God allowed us to remain friends.

When I first started out, my fear was of becoming a cult-like zombie. I certainly didn't want to wear a long flowery skirt or a scarf on my head. I wanted to be me...just not who I was before I met Christ. One thing that keeps me faithful almost 20 years later is remembering who I was without God: bitter, angry, cynical, sarcastic, deceitful and prone to holding grudges. One of the first things my friends and family noticed about me after my baptism was that I actually looked like a different person. When I came to Christ, I looked like I had just stepped off of MTV's Headbangers Ball...think 80s, big hair, little black clothes. Needless to say, I changed the way I dressed. Paul says in I Timothy 2:9-10, "I also want women to dress modestly, with decency and propriety, not with braided hair or gold or pearls or expensive clothes, but with good deeds, appropriate for women who profess to worship God." My new Christian friends suggested a yard sale to help me clear out my closet; but, even I was ashamed to lay most of my clothes out in broad daylight. I just threw them away...and suddenly had nothing to wear. One friend took me shopping in a "regular" store and I didn't even know where to begin; all the clothes were so conservative! It just wasn't "me." Yes, it took time and a lot of loving input to help me understand how to *not* dress provocatively (Colossians 3:12-13).

Modesty is not just about how we dress, but about who we are in what we're wearing. Some clothes make us feel comfortable, some make us feel flirtatious. As a single woman, I needed to learn how to be a friend to men without flirting with them. I literally had to practice looking directly into the eyes of men, rather than up from under my lashes. I had to re-learn how to walk—practicing like a model with a book on her head—without swaying so as to get the attention of everyone I passed. In my mind, I had to walk like I had a stick up my butt. I realize this sounds extreme, but if you are a woman, or a man who knows a woman, you know what I mean and what to watch out for! Some things need to be left behind, literally.

In addition to changing how I dressed and walked, I also needed to change the way I talked. It was easy to quit swearing, but it took the Holy Spirit to help me see the deeper level of cynicism and sarcasm in my heart. One day I was reading Matthew 12:34 about words coming from the overflow of the heart, and suddenly verses 36-37 jumped out at me: "But I tell you that men will have to give account on the day of judgment for every careless word they have spoken. For by your words you will be acquitted, and by your words you will be condemned." It was like God was speaking directly to me." Stop being so sarcastic," he said. I see now that a Christian who can't be funny without negative sarcasm is like the standup comedian who can't do a routine without profanity.

I still listen to rock music, I found my style, and even worked at MTV for several years. I never became a cult-like zombie. Yet, I want to be who I am, not what I was, and so I continue to clean out my closet spiritually on a regular basis. Asking myself these questions really helps: What can I give away (Romans 12:6-8)? What should I throw away (Ephesians 4:31-32)? What will I carry on (II Peter 1:5-8)? What do I need to put in storage (Matthew 6:19-21)? At the end of the day, it doesn't really matter how many boxes we are left with. We have God's promise of "no one who has left home or brothers or sisters or mother or father or children or fields for me and the gospel will fail to receive a hundred times as much in this present age (homes, brothers, sisters, mothers, children and fields—and with them, persecutions) and in the age to come, eternal life" (Mark 10:29-30).

LET IT GO:
What Should I Leave Behind?

Stuff to Talk Through With a Friend
* What are the most noticeable things in my spiritual closet that need to go now?
* Which things in my life will take more time and effort to get rid of because they are entrenched in my heart?
* Who is a Christian I know who has successfully cleaned his or her closet of the same type baggage I have? How did they do it?

Things to Do If You Want to Grow
* Ask a spiritual friend to do an "inventory" of your spiritual closet. Decide what you will get rid of and make a plan with your friend to clean out the things mentioned.

References for Further Bible Study
Proverbs 26:18-20 • Mark 10:17-31 • Corinthians 6:9-20 • II Corinthians 5:15-17 • Romans 6:1-23 • Galatians 2:17-21 • Ephesians 4:1-32 • Colossians 3:1-17 • I John 2:3-17

Additional Resources
The Pursuit of Holiness by Jerry Bridges
The Practice of Godliness by Jerry Bridges
Celebration of Discipline: The Path to Spiritual Growth by Richard J. Foster

For additional resources or to join our online community, go to:
http://fieldguide.faith21.org

13

Let Them Go
Whom Should I Leave Behind?

> *Do not be yoked together with unbelievers. For what do righteousness and wickedness have in common? Or what fellowship can light have with darkness?*
> **II Corinthians 6:14**

When Jesus asks us to leave everything for the sake of the gospel, one of the hardest things to do is to consider that we may have to leave certain relationships behind us. This is a hard but essential question to ask ourselves as Christians. The reality is that, when we decided to make Jesus the Lord of our lives, not many of our friends and family were pleased. Many of us learned a hard truth through rejection and painful conversations: Jesus has many enemies (Philippians 3:18). Sometimes those enemies are the people who are dearest to us. The question hits us: whom should we leave behind?

Questions immediately surface, threatening to confuse the issue. Aren't we supposed to love our enemies (Matthew 5:44)? What about our neighbors; isn't that the second greatest commandment (Mark 12:30)? Didn't Jesus hang out with tax collectors and "sinners" (Luke 7:36-50)? On the other hand, didn't Jesus say to "hate" your father, mother, brother, sister, even your own life (Luke 14:26)? But then Paul says to not love your immediate family is worse than being an unbeliever (I Timothy 5:8)! What if I am "yoked" with an unbeliever (II Corinthians 6:14-18)?

In order to understand the answer to these questions, we must look at the full scope of the Bible's teaching. We know that God does not lie (I Samuel 15:19) and the Bible is solid, right and true (Psalm 119). So all the questions, though troubling, have a solution. Our temptation may be to do nothing, but we must resist that temptation, for this is a great opportunity to be really open with our doubts and feelings. Are we being sentimental rather than reasoning rightly? The Bible says one thing, but our feelings may say something else. The best way to deal with these situations is by using a trusted advisor who can help us see things from a more spiritual perspective (Proverbs 15:22).

When I was studying the Bible and making the decision whether I could make a life-long commitment to Christ, I had to review many of my relationships. I was in a dating relationship at that time that involved heavy drinking, sexual immorality, lying, and anger. Yet, somehow, I thought I was in love. As I started to repent from many of these sins, my relationship began to change. At first, my boyfriend tried to accept this new me, and I hoped he would also desire a relationship with God.

However, as time went on, there were fewer acceptances and more questioning. I will never forget a conversation with him that changed my life forever:

"I love you," he said.

"You do? What does love mean to you?" I wasn't being sarcastic. I had recently learned about God's definition of love (I Corinthians 13) and was curious what he meant by it.

"I don't know, I feel passionate about you," was his

response.

"You do? What does passion mean?"

"I don't know! What does it mean to you?"

"Let's look at the dictionary," I said. At the time, I used to look words up in the dictionary to see what they really meant. I was amazed that many of the words I thought I understood actually meant something very different. I'll never forget the feeling I had as I read Webster's definition: *Passion—The suffering of Jesus at the crucifixion.*[1]

"God loves me," I said in complete shock. I'm sure he was shocked as well. In that moment, I knew that God's love for me was greater than any man's and decided that no relationship is more important than my relationship with him. No one was going to stand between my Lord and me.

The "unequal yoke" of II Corinthians 6:14-18 suddenly made sense. I saw that we no longer had fellowship. Our priorities no longer matched up, and sure enough, the relationship disintegrated. Had I continued with him in our relationship, his values would have become a hindrance to my new life (Hebrews 12:1). In truth, he chose to stay on his same path and I went a different way, so he was naturally left behind. Of course, my desire is that he will find Christ, yet I have accepted that such a conversion will be unlikely to occur through me.

Not every relationship is so black and white. There are many tricky situations which call for a lot of advice from mature Christians. Every situation is unique. However, one thing is sure: our most intimate relationships should be with members of the family of God (Matthew 12:46; Mark 3:31-35; Luke 8:19-21).

Many of my old friends did not choose to follow God.

---

1   http://www.websters-online-dictionary.org/definition/passion

Many of them thought I was going through a "weird phase." As time went on, my world has changed. Since light has no fellowship with darkness, many of my relationships are simply gone. I used to get calls to "go out" and I would gently decline as I knew what that meant with my group of friends. After many years, since they know what my answer will be, the invitations have stopped. It does not mean I am unavailable to my old friends. It just means that I am not willing to partake in things that can cause me to sin.

It wasn't always so clear to me. I have gone to clubs as a Christian, excusing myself by quoting Matthew 9:9-13 and Luke 7:36-50, Jesus hung out with "sinners." However, after close examination of the scriptures, I can clearly see that the intent of these passages is not to give us a license to party irresponsibly with the world. When Jesus ate with the tax collectors and prostitutes, it was not in the brothels or pubs; it was at a Pharisee or disciple's home. The point of these passages is to show us God's grace to everyone (Matthew 21:28-31), not to be used as an excuse to "go out."

Separation naturally follows obedience. Ever since I have separated myself from certain places and things, people have separated themselves from me. As I walk with God, those who choose to walk in the darkness are naturally left behind. Though, of course, they are welcome to follow, and have been invited to do so. We should invite our friends to walk with us in the new way we have chosen to follow, but let us never leave behind our Lord and Savior, Jesus Christ.

LET THEM GO: Whom Should I Leave Behind

Stuff to Talk Through With a Friend
* Who are your closest relationships?
* How have your relationships changed since becoming a Christian?
* How has your family responded to your decision?
* Are there any relationships that have potential to be a stumbling block? If so, what needs to change?

Things to Do If You Want to Grow
* Get advice about any relationships that you question. It's better to walk on the safe side. Many people have wandered from their faith in God due to a certain "friend."
* Spend some time with a mature Christian and talk about your friendships.

References for Further Bible Study
Joshua 24 • Proverbs 20:19, 22:24-25, 23:9, 23:19-22, 24:1-2 • Mark 10:14 • Ephesians 5:1-21, 6:1-4 • II Timothy 1:5 • I Peter 3:1-6

Additional Resources
How People Grow by Dr. Henry Cloud and Dr. John Townsend
Better Together by Rick Warren
Discipled by Jesus by Toney Mulhollan

For additional resources or to join our online community, go to:
http://fieldguide.faith21.org

14

Balance
It Is a Marathon, Not a Sprint

> "The thief comes only to steal and kill and destroy; I have come that they may have life, and have it to the full."
>
> John 10:10

The promise of life to the full speaks to the very core of our beings. When we chose to make Jesus Lord of our lives, it was with the understanding that our lives would finally make sense; that something would be fulfilled in our souls. However, for many Christians, obstacles litter the way to God's promise of life to the full. These Christians have become victims of the thief alluded to in the first part of the aforementioned scripture. So how do we receive the promised life to the full as Christians?

A great place to start would be to take an account of all the activities and responsibilities of your life in list form. Take a piece of paper and write down the general activities of your life. Don't worry about it being perfect, just jot down whatever activities come to mind.

Now, if your list is like mine, it reveals a very busy person. Most of us are juggling more responsibilities than we can effectively handle. We run around trying to accomplish daily tasks that have nothing to do with our dreams. Even as Christians, the things that we know are important to God seem to get reduced to a list of spiritual chores. When did the promise of "life to the full" transform to "life crammed with activity?" Sometimes, we are just trying to survive the day, trying to get by without too many difficulties, rather than striving to glorify God by living excellent lives filled with peace, joy and love. Are our friends in the world attracted to this type of stressful life?

The problem for most of us is that we tend to focus on the things that are easy, most interesting, or simply whatever is right in front of us. We neglect some things that are really important and, before we know it, we start to feel a little harassed and unbalanced. We feel incomplete but we don't know what is missing. The real problem is that the things we have neglected diminish our strengths and make us unfruitful. The dreams and goals we long to accomplish are unrealized, not because of some external opposition, but because we have not taken care of some key areas of our lives. We shoot ourselves in the foot and wonder why we limp. Eventually, our lives may lead us to say what Solomon espouses in Ecclesiastes 2:1: "Everything is meaningless."

In summary, we will never have the life to the full that Jesus promised, until we achieve a life of balance. If we spend our lives chasing after the unimportant, though seemingly very urgent things, we will never achieve a spiritually fulfilling and abundant life.

How can we live healthy, balanced lives in this world that is constantly clamoring for attention? Following are seven steps that will help get us there:

Step 1 - Identify the problem

God is offering us a balanced life to the full and we are the ones messing it up.

Step 2 - Develop a sense of urgency

As Christians, we believe in the resurrection of the dead, not in reincarnation. We've got ONE CHANCE at this life here on Earth! How urgent are you about living the rest of your life to your fullest potential?

The parable of the talents shows us what urgency in life looks like. One servant squandered his opportunity to be successful and chose to let fear give him a mediocre life. The other servants heard those incredible words of validation: "Well done, good and faithful servant! You have been faithful with a few things; I will put you in charge of many things. Come and share your master's happiness" (Matthew 25:14-30)! Will you choose right now to share in your master's happiness?

Step 3 - Know what balance looks like

The following seven key areas encapsulate much of what God wants to give us in our lives.

  * **Relationship with God** (Psalm 127:1; Matthew 22:36-38)
    Your relationship with God should be the most important relationship you invest in. The fruits of the Spirit should provide evidence of this in your life.

  * **Relationships with friends and family** (I Timothy 5:8; Matthew 22:39)
    We can't claim to be close to God and yet hate our fellow man.

  * **Service to the church** (I Corinthians 12:4-31)
    The church is the body of Christ. What part do you play?

* **Work and finances** (Colossians 3:23; Proverbs 11:24-25, 21:20)
  How we make and spend our money says much about our priorities.
* **Caring for your own body** (I Corinthians 6:19-20)
  Our diet, exercise and sleep habits affect the work the Holy Spirit in us can do.
* **Times of rest** (Mark 2:27)
  Rest keeps us from burning out. Remember that life is a marathon, not a sprint.
* **Have fun** (I Timothy 6:17)
  God created this world to be enjoyed.

We must realize that whenever any one of these areas becomes dysfunctional, it will impact the *whole of our lives*. We must not neglect these key components of a balanced life.

Step 4 - Identify where your life is out of balance
Look at the order of your list of daily activities. It will tell you something about what's on the forefront of your mind. Ask someone who knows you well if your life is balanced.

Step 5 - Identify why your weaknesses remain
The reason may be one of the following:
  * You've been unaware of your areas of needed development
  * You've been lazy
  * You've been afraid
  * You've been prideful
  * You've been indifferent
  * You've been unequipped

Remember how it says in John 10:10 that the *thief* comes to steal and kill and destroy. Who is the thief? Satan is the obvious answer, but sometimes he barely needs to lift a finger. We often do his work for him. Our ignorance, fear, pride or indifference robs us of God's promises.

Step 6 - Tackle one weakness at a time

If we try to take on too much at once, we can become overwhelmed and give up. Deal with the most pressing issue first, invite accountability, seek counsel and see it through until growth is noticeable. Then move on to the next area of development.

Step 7 - Never, ever quit!

…until you hear the words, "Well done, my good and faithful servant…well done" (Matthew 25:21).

BALANCE:
It Is a Marathon, Not a Sprint

Stuff to Talk Through With a Friend
* What areas in my life seem to be out of balance?
* What traits in my character are keeping me from growing in this area?
* How has my unbalanced lifestyle affected my relationships with people?
* How will my unbalanced lifestyle affect my relationship with God in the long-term?

Things to Do If You Want to Grow
* Go through the steps outlined in this chapter.
* Seek council regarding what you have been neglecting.
* Invite accountability.

References for Further Bible Study
The book of Ecclesiastes

Additional Resources
Finding Balance by Sheila Jones (for women)
Living the Spiritually Balanced Life by Ray S. Anderson
Balanced Christian Life by Stephen Kaung
Benedict's Way: An Ancient Monk's Insights for a Balanced Life by Daniel Homan
The Power of Discipling by Gordon Ferguson

For additional resources or to join our online community, go to:
http://fieldguide.faith21.org

15

God's Discipline
Considering It Pure Joy

> *And he said: "I tell you the truth, unless you change and become like little children, you will never enter the kingdom of heaven. Therefore, whoever humbles himself like this child is the greatest in the kingdom of heaven."*
> Matthew 18:3-4

Correction is never fun. It challenges who we are, what we've done, choices we've made and tests our character. How we respond when God disciplines us will make or break us as Christians. Consider Jesus' words in Matthew 18 about the humility of children. Children are a great picture of what it means to be humble; they are usually teachable and will listen to the authority in their lives. Unfortunately, when we become adults, we have a much harder time being humble. Our emotions, insecurities and even achievements get in the way of a child-like humility.

If we have a hard time being humble when God is trying to correct and discipline us, we will find ourselves on the losing side of a battle for our spiritual lives. When Jesus speaks of unconditional surrender in Luke 14:31-33, he is not merely referring to becoming a Christian, he is speaking of our continual walk as disciples of Jesus. As God brings correction and discipline into our lives, we must continue to be unconditionally surrendered to his will for our lives. We have to maintain a spirit of complete willingness to give up everything for him. No area of our lives is outside of God's discipline. He wants to direct us in how we spend our time, how we spend money, our relationships, our work ethic, our marriage, how we respond to authority and our choices in general.

I remember God using people to bring discipline and correction into my life during my early years as a Christian. Each time, the outcome hinged upon my humility to let go of what I thought about my life, and my willingness to embrace God's will. I would often find myself seeking guidance in the book of Proverbs, with passages like these:

> "Trust in the Lord with all your heart and lean not on your own understanding." Proverbs 3:5

> "My son, do not despise the Lord's discipline and do not resent his rebuke, because the Lord disciplines those he loves, as a father the son he delights in." Proverbs 3:11-12

> "When pride comes, then comes disgrace, but with humility comes wisdom." Proverbs 11:2

> "The way of a fool seems right to him, but a wise man listens to advice." Proverbs 12:15

If you are in a season of God's discipline, the most important question you have to answer is: "Whom will I trust?" There are only two choices: God or yourself. These two answers take you down very different paths, so it is crucial to understand what they look like and how we go about making those choices.

Hebrews 12:2 gives us great insight into accepting God's discipline. It says, "Let us fix our eyes on Jesus, the author and perfecter of our faith, who for the joy set before him endured the cross, scorning its shame and sat down at the right hand of the throne of God." Actually, this whole chapter offers us a wise perspective on how to look at God's discipline in our lives. The key is to keep our eyes on Jesus. It's so easy to focus on our circumstances, our pain, and ourselves in general when facing discipline. However, the writer of Hebrews reminds us to stay focused on Jesus; when we do, it puts our problems in perspective. We see Jesus facing incredible challenges, and yet coming out on the other side victorious. Jesus left us with a supreme example when he focused on the promise of God instead of the daunting reality of the cross. At times, we can become so consumed with the discipline we are facing that we forget God's promises and feel overwhelmed and without hope. Hebrews 12:5-11 reminds us that, while God's discipline is not pleasant, it holds the promise to train us in righteousness and give us peace. This promise depends on our submission to him and our willingness to be trained by his discipline.

What has God put in your life recently to discipline you? What choices are you making? Do you trust God or are you trusting your emotions? God loves you dearly, but he is far more interested in your character than in your comfort. He wants you to make it to Heaven and spend eternity with him, but knows that if you don't accept his discipline on Earth, you will miss out on eternity. That is why this issue is so crucial for all of us to embrace. If we reject God's discipline and choose the path of trusting ourselves over God and his people, we will be led down a dark path of self-centered thinking that few have ever returned from.

The past few years have brought this teaching to life for

me. First my wife and then I have been asked to come out of the full-time ministry in our church. Through it all, I have constantly battled my own insecurities about our future and God's plan for our lives. I struggled to trust the godly people in my life who had loved me for years and to not give in to my emotions. As I wrestled with my own insecurities, I found myself before God time and time again fighting to choose whom I would trust—myself or God. God would remind me of how much people had loved me, all that he'd done in my life up to that point; that he was still the boss of me and had greater things to come if I would only trust him.

We all need to realize that God always disciplines us for a reason and there is a plan in all of it. Someone recently commented, "God has not forgotten me but is preparing me." I love that sentiment because it is so true; but it will help us only if we choose to believe it. Consider how God is disciplining you right now and imagine what he is preparing you for. Believe and trust that he loves you very much and has your best interests in mind. Only when we trust God's discipline, will we have true joy, peace and contentment in his will for our lives.

GOD'S DISCIPLINE:
Considering It Pure Joy

Stuff to Talk Through With a Friend
* In what ways has God disciplined me in the past? Is he disciplining me now?
* Do I learn from God's corrections? Or does God discipline me for the same thing over and over again?
* Do I trust the brothers and sisters in my life?

Things to Do If You Want to Grow
* Pray that God would show you any areas in your life that you have not surrendered to him. Ask those who know you if you live a surrendered life.
* Tell God that you want his discipline. Really tell him that you want it.
* Ask others in your life for examples where God has disciplined them and what they learned from it.

References for Further Bible Study
Deuteronomy 8:5 • Job 5:17 • Proverbs 1, 3:1-18, 12:1 •
I Corinthians 11:32 • Revelation 3:19

Additional Resources
The Power of Suffering: Strengthening Your Faith in the Refiner's Fire by John MacArthur
Refined by Fire by Gordon Ferguson

16

Openness
Walking in the Light

> *When Jesus spoke again to the people, he said, "I am the light of the world. Whoever follows me will never walk in darkness, but will have the light of life."*
>
> John 8:12

I was doing my best to hold back tears. My new friend had just shared a story that cut straight to my heart. "Thank you so much for sharing that with me. I can totally relate to your story. In fact, almost the whole time you were talking, especially about your father, I was trying not to cry."

"Yes, but the whole time I was telling you that story you had a smile on your face. That's how deceitful you are!" Tears I had been choking back started to flow. My friend continued, "I am sure you are open about the things you know you should be, like confessing obvious sins, but I bet you are not open about the deep things of your heart. You never learned how to be."

This story was in response to my concern about plateauing spiritually. I had come to a standstill in my walk and my friend was sharing that the answer to my spiritual state was overcoming my fears through deep openness.

The advice all tied into I John 1:5-10:

> *This is the message we have heard from him and declare to you: God is light; in him there is no darkness at all. If we claim to have fellowship with him yet walk in the darkness, we lie and do not live by the truth. But if we walk in the light, as he is in the light, we have fellowship with one another, and the blood of Jesus, his Son, purifies us from all sin. If we claim to be without sin, we deceive ourselves and the truth is not in us. If we confess our sins, he is faithful and just and will forgive us our sins and purify us from all unrighteousness. If we claim we have not sinned, we make him out to be a liar and his word has no place in our lives.*

We give Satan a stronghold in our hearts and sacrifice true fellowship with God and others when we keep things in the dark. We will never truly experience freedom from sin and fear until we make the decision to bring everything, no matter how ugly, unpopular or embarrassing, into the light. We must come clean even if we fear what people might think; that no one will like us if they know who we really are. These fears are the playthings of Satan, the father of lies (John 8:43-45). The way out of this trap is to focus on pleasing God rather than man (Psalm 27:1, 56:11, 118:6; Ephesians 6:12; Hebrews 13:5-6). It is true that someone may occasionally judge or think unkindly of us for being open, but the majority of Christians will relate to our battles and reassure us that we are not alone.

We all struggle. We all have weaknesses. We have been there and probably will be there again at some point—that is why we need Jesus and each other. Many Christians have traveled this path before us and can teach us what helped them to overcome (II Corinthians 1:3-5; Hebrews 13:7). Only when we bring things into the light will we have reinforcements in the battle, to pray for us, to hold us accountable and help us to repent (James 5:15-16; I John 1:9). We are not strong enough to fight the battle alone.

Don't underestimate daily spiritual warfare. Rarely do people leave God because of a sudden catastrophe. Falling away usually starts by ignoring the pricking of our conscience. We choose to not confess, to tell a lie or to hold back the truth—and start down the path of darkness. Along the way, our hearts harden and we lose our conscience (Psalm 36:3; Romans 1:21-22). What we think is no big deal is actually the beginning of a slow, spiritual death as Satan lures us from the light into the darkness (Jeremiah 9:6). Unless there is radical repentance, it will destroy us spiritually.

So how do we live in the light? My friend gave me some of the best practical advice I have ever received: "The very thing you don't want to tell someone the most, needs to be the first thing you say to them." Are you hoping someone won't ask you a certain question? *You* be the one to bring it up. Do you catch yourself lying? Go back and apologize. Has someone hurt your feelings? Tell them even if it might embarrass you. Confess temptation *before* you commit a sin. Radical? Yes, maybe, unless you consider what's at stake. Humiliating? It can be. But boy, do you get that conscience back quickly; and pretty soon, you are much more careful about giving in to deceit.

When we are open, we start to break free from loneliness. Before we do, we may think we are the only ones that feel or think the way we do. That is exactly what Satan wants us to believe. It is only when we choose to bring things into the light that we see we are not alone. It brings us closer together and deepens our friendships. We see more clearly in the light and can experience the kind of fellowship that God wants for us (I John 1:7); the kind of fellowship that brings freedom. Our choice to bring things into the light is a powerful weapon in the spiritual battle.

So why do we fight openness? It goes back to the struggle between the spirit and the flesh (Romans 8:5-9). Each time we choose the light, our spirit gets stronger; likewise, each time we choose to hide in the dark, our flesh gets stronger. We cannot serve two masters; we either live in darkness or light. Whom will we follow: the prince of darkness or the Father of the heavenly lights? It is a daily, sometimes hourly, decision we need to make over and over—but never forget this constant decision is a matter of life and death (Romans 8:13).

Confession and openness will bring our lives into the light, where the battle is often won or lost. Confession is, of course, only the first step in walking in the light. Once things are brought into the light, we must repent of sin and seek to live like Jesus. I John 2:4-6 states, "The man who says, 'I know him,' but does not do what he commands is a liar, and the truth is not in him...Whoever claims to live in him must walk as Jesus did." Jesus always walked in the light.

OPENNESS:
Walking in the Light

Stuff to Talk Through With a Friend
* When reading this, is there anything that came to mind you need to be open about?
* Is there a sin that you have been keeping hidden?
* Are there things you are afraid that people will find out about you?
* Are there things that you are afraid to talk to people about?
* Are there things about the Bible, God, etc. that you don't understand and are ashamed to ask anyone about?

Things to Do If You Want to Grow
* Is there anyone you need to confront, forgive, reconcile with or apologize to (I John 2:9-11)? Get advice and do it.
* Ask three people close to you if they think you are open and vulnerable.
* Study out deceit, honesty and pleasing God versus man in the Bible.

References for Further Bible Study
Psalm 5:6, 101:7 • Proverbs 26:23-28 • Ecclesiastes 2:13 • Zephaniah 3:13 • John 3:20, 8:12 • Romans 8:1-17, 13:12 • Colossians 1:13 • II Timothy 3:13 • I Peter 3:10 • I John 1 and 2

Additional Resources
The Calvary Road by Roy Hession

For additional resources or to join our online community, go to:
http://fieldguide.faith21.org

17

Accountability
You Can't Go It Alone

> *The way of a fool seems right to him,*
> *but a wise man listens to advice.*
> **Proverbs 12:15**

The dictionary defines being accountable as "liable to being called to account; answerable."

How do you feel when you read this definition? Does it make you think of words like "control-freak," "overbearing" or maybe even "back off?" When I think of accountability, I think of opportunity and grace, but I did not always think this way. Even after 13 years of being a Christian, I still sometimes regress to a natural dislike of accountability. But I have experienced a transformation in mindset that did not evolve from my own goodness; rather, it was shaped by the Word, prayer, experience and friends. I had to learn how to be humble before I was able to learn how to be accountable. Keep humility in mind as we walk through this chapter. Accountability will not work without humility.

Like many of the latch-key kids raised in the 80s and 90s, I came and went as I wished, while mom and dad were at work.

My experiences taught me how to entertain myself and occupy my time. Unfortunately, these experiences also nurtured rebellion and independence, traits which have stayed with me well into my adult years. At times, during the lonely days of my upbringing, independence served me well. As a Christian, it has not. I have often made independent and rebellious decisions that have caused me and other people pain. As I look back over those decisions, it's easy to see what mistakes I made, and what I would change if I were in the same situation today. My sins encompassed immorality, smoking marijuana and walking away from God for over three years. I share this information to my shame. At those times, I chose not to be open or accountable to the people in my life (Proverbs 15:22). I was not using the avenues God provided for my being open about what was really going on in my heart. I was cheating God, myself, and the brothers and sisters in my life. Friends made themselves available to me, but I had not made my heart available to them. How could they know what was going on? How could they help me with challenges when I kept deep sins in the dark? I was not letting God shed light in the scary places of my heart. Thankfully, the Holy Spirit always knows what's going on. Even if we hide it from others, nothing is hidden from God (Ecclesiastes 12:14; I Corinthians 4:5). In those times of darkness, God used people to talk to me, but I would harden my heart and deflect or blame-shift. I did this so often as a young Christian that it took me out, and I walked away! My heart hardened and my faith waned. Sin's deceitfulness had me in its clutches. I spent three years in the desert, with God hard on my case. Only with my life in ruins around me did I eventually let God shine the light on who I really was and what I had been doing.

Independence slowly erodes at the reliance we should have

on God. Many of God's people in the Bible fell short of his glory due to independence and rebellion. They could have avoided many of their mistakes had they been accountable. The same goes for us. Please, do not test God on this. Make a decision to let people in your life today (Proverbs 27:12).

Following are some ideas on how to let people in your life, heart and mind. The first is to renew our minds (Romans 12:2). Someone once said, "A mind is a dangerous place. You don't want to go in there alone." Without God, our minds become corrupt and need renewal. We have memories of sins from our past as well as ideas and philosophies that conflict with God's word. If we want to align our thoughts with the Word of God, we must first read and study it (Joshua 1:8). This process is not easy. Thankfully, if we are unclear about something, we can always seek advice or counsel from a close friend to give us clarity on a situation (Proverbs 15:22).

Memorizing scriptures to help in areas where we are weak or would like to grow in is also very beneficial (Psalm 119:93). Areas of study may include marriage, finances, purity and character. In addition to scripture, we can also join groups that help in these particular areas. A chemical recovery group can help a person learn to live comfortably without using drugs or alcohol. A marriage group can give couples a new perspective on how to have a healthy marriage. Groups that deal with impurity will help us stand out in a society that does not choose to protect or value purity. These are just a few of the various groups we can be accountable to in order to allow people to help spiritually transform our mind and heart. Spiritual people can instill countless invaluable concepts, perspectives and ideas into our lives that we might miss if we just relied on our own good judgment or feelings. Whatever your need and situation, there are plenty of spiritual groups and classes that can help you shore up your convictions and spiritual walk.

Having a small number of close friends who have similar spiritual beliefs, morals, and convictions is a great tool for spiritual growth (I Corinthians 15:33). Not every one of your advisors needs to agree with you, as it is a good idea to have people in our lives who are willing to disagree or confront us (Proverbs 27:6). However, make sure that the people you are listening to are following the Bible and God's instruction. This is a more difficult task than it seems at times. Many of us have family members or friends whom we deeply connect with and love, but may not wish to emulate. No need to exclude them from your handful of advisors; just make sure you incorporate righteous people as your mainstay.

As you begin to put these principles into action, you can expect opposition (Nehemiah 4:11). Thankfully, you can also expect God to bless your efforts as you draw near to him (James 4:8). Looking back, how I wish I would have used these tools as a young Christian! Not being accountable to the people in my life was my downfall. You now have the same opportunity I had, but you can make better choices than I did in my early years. May God be with you as you open up your life to his light!

ACCOUNTABILITY: You Can't Go It Alone

Stuff to Talk Through With a Friend
* Can I be entirely open with my sins, weaknesses and failures with my good friends?
* Who are the friends I am accountable to? Is it enough?
* Am I holding somebody else accountable to spiritual growth?
* Do I ask for advice when faced with decisions in my life? If not, what excuses do I use?

Things to Do If You Want to Grow
* Consider carefully the closest friendships in your life. Are you able to be open with them? If not, then work through any issues.
* If you do not have close friendships you can be accountable to, ask somebody you respect if they would have that relationship with you.
* Get together with your close friend(s) every week and ask each other specific questions that will help you grow and repent of sin.

References for Further Bible Study
Exodus 18:19 • I Samuel 16:20 • I Kings 12:8 • II Chronicles 10:8 • Esther 1:21 • Proverbs 13:10, 19:20, 20:18 • Daniel 4:27 • Acts 27:11, 27:21 • II Corinthians 8:10

Additional Resources
The Accountable Man: Pursuing Integrity Through Trust and Friendship by Tom L. Eisenman
The Art of Christian Listening by Thomas N. Hart
Love One Another by Gordon Ferguson
One Another by Tom Jones and Steve Brown

For additional resources or to join our online community, go to:
http://fieldguide.faith21.org

18

Victory!
Against All Odds

And that is what some of you were. But you were washed, you were sanctified, you were justified in the name of the Lord Jesus Christ and by the Spirit of our God.
I Corinthians 6:11

Rock bottom. I will never forget the utter despair I felt on this particular night as I left yet another secret gay hangout I frequented. Almost a decade of anonymous homosexual encounters, living a double life, lying to those I was close to out of fear I'd hurt them, and the break-up of a long-term relationship had all taken its toll. I knew I couldn't live like this any longer.

Ultimately, I didn't have the strength to stop this thing that I loved; this thing that I hated. The more I indulged myself, the emptier I felt. I would continue the same behavior to get my "fix," hoping to numb the pain, even temporarily. It was a vicious cycle. Not a very victorious story so far, is it?

Thank God this wasn't the final chapter in my life. In spite of the seemingly insurmountable odds that were stacked against me, the Lord lovingly gave me hope and a future. He sent me godly men who loved me regardless of who I had become. They saw my sin as equal to any other, and in them, I experienced God's compassion. Finally, seeing hope in what I had believed was a hopeless situation, I quickly repented, quit my gay lifestyle forever and decided to follow Jesus.

That old life is now decades behind me. Since becoming a Christian, God has blessed me with a loving wife of 20 years, four great kids and a continuous sense of God's grace in my life.

I am no longer a slave to homosexuality and celebrate the freedom I have in Christ to choose the path of self-denial and obedience to God. It is about making daily choices (Romans 6:15-22). Homosexuality used to have control over me, but I now have control over it. This is the kind of victory that we can all experience, regardless of the nature of our challenges, with the help of God. Everything Satan has meant for evil, God can use for good. We are not victims, we are a part of the solution to a lost and dying world; and this is how God has turned my weakness into my strength (II Corinthians 12:8-10).

In order to survive, let alone successfully live, as a Christian for the long term, we must be able to overcome our trials in spite of severe difficulties. The Bible is full of such stories where, no matter the odds, the person overcomes. In the one that we are going to consider briefly, the Holy Spirit uses a word full of optimism and tenacity: "nevertheless."

> "The king and his men marched to Jerusalem to attack the Jebusites, who lived there. The Jebusites said to David, 'You will not get in here; even the blind and the lame can ward you off.' They thought, 'David cannot get in here.' Nevertheless, David captured the fortress of Zion, the City of David."
>
> II Samuel 5: 6-7

By this time, David had just been crowned king. His first order of business was to take Jerusalem by force from the Jebusites, who had occupied the city for the previous 400 years. Relocating to Jerusalem was a strategic move; it provided David not only with a strong citadel militarily, but also a neutral site politically, lying on the border between Judah and the Northern Tribes.

The problem facing David, however, was that Jerusalem was a veritable fortress. The city had high, thick walls that were considered unscalable. Additionally, the Jebusites were known as a brutally tough nation, especially skilled in war and celebrated for their bravery.

David's army, on the other hand, was small and would have been outmanned, out-skilled and considered a weakling militarily. No wonder the enemy was so convinced of its own superiority.

On that historic day when David and his tiny militia showed up for battle, the Jebusites looked over the wall, scoffed at them and said in effect, "You scum have been trying for 400 years to get past these walls, but look at you; you're such a pathetic little army; even our lame and blind people could defeat you."

And then in II Samuel 5:7 comes one of the greatest sentences in the entire Bible; a decree that screams out what one man can do against enormous odds when God is on his side. It is a verdict that should fill us with lifelong optimism; a declaration that should give us strength during our times of adversity. The Bible simply states, "Nevertheless, David captured the fortress of Zion."

So short was the battle. So quickly did the strong and brave fall. So overwhelmingly powerful was David's Israelite army that the Holy Spirit did not think it necessary to bother recording what happened next. The obstacles were enormous, but so was David's faith, and so was God's help.

We each have our own fortified cities to storm. We have character changes to make. We suffer doubts about our abilities to stay faithful. Some of us have struggled with the same sin for so long, we see no light at the end of the tunnel. We transgress and hurt ourselves. Satan constantly attacks, and the world continually calls. We must also contend with real-life, everyday problems like physical ailments, companies downsizing and bills mounting. Some may ask, "Where is the victory in this?"

Yet, God calls out to each one of us through examples like David to show us that, "nevertheless," he will fight for us. We can tear down the walls of our own fortified cities, for we follow a God who does his best work when the chance for victory seems impossible.

By God's grace, I was rescued from the bondage of living a life of homosexuality. Satan had built such a wall around that sin, I couldn't imagine being set free. Yet here I am; liberated! What has Satan been telling you is impossible to change? Do the odds seem stacked against you? Great! God is eager to rescue you. You can overcome and be victorious, nevertheless!

VICTORY!: Against All Odds

Stuff to Talk Through With a Friend

* Can you give an example from your life where you made a dramatic change, and share how you did this?
* Do you see any opportunities for repentance in your life, character flaws, sinful thought patterns or activities?

Things to Do If You Want to Grow

* What "fortified walls" still exist in your heart that you have not turned over to God, allowing him to bring about victory in your life? Sit down in a quiet place, and after praying for God's revelation, write out your thoughts.
* Godly victory over any broken area of our lives is impossible without authentic and honest transparency with God and other trusted Christian friends (James 5:13-20). What areas of your life have you kept hidden in the darkness for fear of what others might think or say? Ask God to reveal these to you, then ask a mature and trusted Christian companion to walk by your side in prayer and accountability as you tear down this wall that Satan has been building. If you don't yet know of anyone with whom you feel is a safe and secure person with whom to speak, pray daily that the Lord will lead you to this individual.
* Remember, there is no glory in quitting. Stay resolute and focused on God's grace when you suffer setbacks, trusting that his grace is sufficient (II Corinthians 12:9), and then get up and try again (Proverbs 24:16).
* Be patient with the Holy Spirit who will move according to his timing, not yours. As long as you are consistently praying, striving for daily purity and righteousness and allowing people to help you, victory will come!

References for Further Bible Study

II Kings 6:8-22 • Hebrews 1:14 • II Chronicles 19:1-2 • Exodus 14 • Psalm 46:10 • I Corinthians 6:9-11

Additional Resources

Mind Change: A Biblical Path to Overcoming Life's Challenges by Thomas A. Jones
Desires in Conflict: Hope for Men Who Struggle with Sexual Identity by Joe Dallas
The Heart of Female Same-Sex Attraction by Janelle Hallman
Strength in Weakness Ministries (www.strengthinweakness.org)

19

Sexual Purity
Overcoming a Multi-Faced Sin

> *Do you not know that your body is a temple of the Holy Spirit,*
> *who is in you, whom you have received from God?*
> *You are not your own; you were bought at a price.*
> *Therefore honor God with your body.*
> I Corinthians 6:19-20

When I was 11, I sat in a public restroom and perused a stack of pornographic magazines left behind. For the first time, a "buzz" feeling of lust raced through my body and soul. That "buzz" filled the awkwardness of being a child who was looking for significance in the world and acceptance from the influential adults around me. Pornography seemed to fulfill those desires during those early years. I learned early in life that when I was feeling lonely, angry, incompetent, tired, sad, disrespected or ineffective, the buzz was just one indulgence away and it would soothe my pain. For me, it came in all forms, from dozens of promiscuous relationships where I felt a form of love and admiration, to pornography delivered in print, on television or through the Internet.

When I became a Christian, I assumed that, with the new Holy Spirit in me, I would automatically overcome my sexual sins. *I did not* (II Peter 2:19). What is it that makes some of us continue to struggle with lust or self-gratification or pornography, or promiscuous relationships or worse? It is more than just our understanding of morality or our lack of desire to be righteous (Psalms 19:13). It is because we are *deeply lonely*. We feel alone and feel that our very lives depend on removing that loneliness any way we can.

Proverbs 19:22 says, "What a man desires is unfailing love; better to be poor than a liar." God installed in the soul of every man and woman an eternal desire for unfailing love, manifested through acceptance, emotional nourishment, meaning, intimacy, friendship and security. Our desire for love is not the problem; the problem is that we look for (and settle for) *false love*. For some of us, we find this false love in our careers, relationships, money or other passions that might seem harmless to the world, but are unhealthy for our souls. For example, we might habitually numb out through television, or have a strategic glass of wine, or feel empowered and admired by excessive work. We might eat to comfort a painful emotion or find security through financial success (I John 2:15-16; Proverbs 5:22).

In John 4:10-18, Jesus uses water to illustrate the difference between God's unfailing love and false love. He meets a woman at a well, and explains that she can either drink the water in that well and be thirsty again, or she can drink from the "Living Water" of Christ and be fulfilled for eternity. She had five husbands and was well on her way to number six by the time she met Jesus at the well. She knew the shortcomings of false love.

As Christians, we cannot continue to pursue these false loves. Ephesians 1:4 says, "[God] chose us in him before the creation of the world to be holy and blameless in his sight." Paul says in Romans 12:1, "Therefore, I urge you, brothers, in view of God's mercy, to offer your bodies as living sacrifices, holy and pleasing to God—this is your spiritual act of worship. Again, even more clearly in Ephesians 5:3, "But among you there must not be even a hint of sexual immorality, or of any kind of impurity, or of greed, because these are improper for God's holy people." We repented from our sin and now we must see this repentance through to the end (Matthew 3:8).

The Answer: Intimacy

Knowing we must continually repent does not rid us of the guilt over our behavior (Romans 7:15-21), nor does it fill our need for true love. Our hearts must be filled with an unfailing love in order to break the sinful cycle of searching for love in the wrong places. This unfailing love comes in the form of *intimacy* with God and other people.

The definition of intimacy is "to know and be known." The first half of Proverbs 19:22 states that we are all searching for *"unfailing love."* But the second half says, "…better to be poor than a liar." It is better to be truly known, even if we are poor and wretched, than to lie about who we are, not letting God and the people close to us know the deepest parts of our soul. Letting God and a few others into those areas of our soul soothes that aching loneliness and fulfills our relentless search for unfailing love.

Intimacy goes hand in hand with confession. Through deep confession to God and a few like-minded Christians, intimacy is created. Confession isn't about listing our sins to God and others and then feeling guilty about them. It is about admitting not only what we've done, but also the events that led up to it and our hearts behind it. If we can identify *why* we sinned, we can identify the triggers that Satan uses to tempt us. We can then stop the cycle of sin when we feel these triggers being pulled (James 1:15).

Many times, these triggers that tempt us to sin come from wounds of our past. Perhaps we feel *incompetent* at work because we made a mistake. We want to alleviate the pain of that perceived incompetence or humiliation and so turn to pornography and masturbation. Perhaps we feel *insignificant*—like we don't matter—so we flirt with someone who makes us feel better about ourselves. Maybe we feel *powerless*—we can't seem to change our careers or relationships for the better. So we look at pornography or eat a whole box of cookies because we believe we have power over what we feel and when and how we decide. When confessing to your small group of friends, and to God, be on the lookout for these triggers and talk about them openly. Discuss ways to avoid these triggers or to work through them.

Our short-term goal is to repent from impurity in whatever form through some practical tools listed below. Our long-term goal is to fulfill our need for unfailing love through an ever-deepening intimacy with God and a few friends. This intimacy with God and others will extinguish the sinful desires of our old natures. Finding true love is the only way.

SEXUAL PURITY:
Overcoming a Multi-Faced Sin

Stuff to Talk Through With a Friend
* What are some "false loves" in my life?
* Do I have at least 2-3 friends who know me intimately?
* Have I had a really sincere and deeply intimate prayer with God lately (Psalms 51:10-17)?
* Am I willing to wholeheartedly use the practical tools listed above for six months (I Corinthians 9:26-27)?

Things to Do If You Want to Grow
* Commit to reading your Bible and praying each day in order to grow in your intimacy with God.
* Immediately eliminate all accessibility to pornography, inappropriate relationships and all temptations that trigger related sins. This might include getting Internet accountability software on your computer(s), parental controls on your TVs, getting a new job to avoid a co-worker or finding a new route to work to avoid an adult business (Matthew 5:29).
* Get into or start a weekly discussion group, which specifically and solely discusses sexual behavior. Talk about your sins from the past week, what led up to them and your heart behind them. And most importantly, discuss strategies for the upcoming week to avoid this sin. Hold each other accountable to these strategies each week (II Corinthians 4:2).
* Meet with a spiritually like-minded and same-gender peer each week. Write out a small list of accountability questions ahead of time which specifically address your individual triggers and usual sins and have this person ask you these questions each week (Proverbs 29:25).
* Write out a list of reasons and/or motivational phrases to help overcome sexual sin. Read this list every day.
* If needed, see a Christian therapist to help overcome deeper, on-going emotional needs that trigger these behaviors.

SEXUAL PURITY:
Overcoming a Multi-Faced Sin cont...

References for Further Bible Study
* Intimacy with God: Psalm 139:1-6, 139:23-24; I Peter 1:3-8; Lamentations 3:21-26, 3:31-32; Psalms 19:12-14
* Purity: I Peter 1:16
* Reality Check: Matthew 5:28; Proverbs 6:26
* Repentance: Romans 13:11-14; John 14:15; II Corinthians 7:10-11
* Perseverance: James 1:12; Romans 8:31-39

Additional Resources
The Game Plan: The Men's 30-Day Strategy for Attaining Sexual Integrity by Joe Dallas

Breaking Free: Understanding Sexual Addiction & the Healing Power of Jesus by Russell Willingham

Healing for Damaged Emotions: Recovering from the Memories That Cause Our Pain by David Seamands

Tactics: Securing the Victory in Every Young Man's Battle by Fred Stoeker with Mike Yorkey

Every Heart Restored: A Wife's Guide to Healing in the Wake of a Husband's Sexual Sin by Stephen Arterburn, Fred Stoeker, Brenda Stoeker

Every Woman's Battle by Shannon Ethridge

XXXChurch.com

InternetSafety.com—"Safe Eyes" accountability software (MAC & PC & iPhone)

Pure in Heart by David Weidner

Building a Pure Marriage in an Impure World by David and Robin Weidner

Pursuing Purity by Virginia Lefler

For additional resources or to join our online community, go to:
http://fieldguide.faith21.org

20

Spiritual Warfare
There's a Target on Your Back

> *Be self-controlled and alert. Your enemy the devil prowls around like a roaring lion looking for someone to devour. Resist him, standing firm in the faith, because you know that your brothers throughout the world are undergoing the same kind of sufferings.*
> **I Peter 5:8-9**

My co-worker would have thought our conversation ordinary, but the impact on me couldn't have been more profound. The topic of the devil somehow came up, and I mentioned that I didn't believe there was a Satan, as the concept seemed so primitive. My companion floored me by replying, "That's interesting. Jesus believed in Satan." Even with my rudimentary knowledge of the Bible at the time, I realized my ignorance. Clearly, I had a lot to learn from Jesus about divine warfare. So began my quest for greater spiritual understanding.

Most people today are as ignorant as I was. Recently, a survey in *Christianity Today* reported that only about 1/3 of American Christians believe Satan is real.[1] He has done a masterful job in convincing most of us that there really isn't

---

[1] http://in.christiantoday.com/articles/most-us-christians-don-believe-satan-holy-spirit-exist/3704.htm

an evil force in the world. What a huge advantage Satan has gained by making so many unaware of whom they're battling against in the war for their souls! Regardless of what we believe, Satan is alive and should be respected and feared. Revelation 12:10, describes Satan's loss to God in a battle of the heavenly realms, taking the fallen angels with him, and his eviction from heaven. A few verses later in Revelation 12:12, God reveals to us, "But woe to the earth and the sea, because the devil has gone down to you! He is filled with fury, because he knows that his time is short." Satan realizes that he has a limited time to strike back. Lashing out by separating as many people from God as possible is his venomous retaliation.

His weapons are formidable and yet predictable. The Apostle Paul was wary of Satan's plans when he noted, "For we are not unaware of his schemes" (II Corinthians 2:10-11). God compares Satan's attacks to a lion on the prowl (I Peter 5:8-9). Lions will wait in disguise as long as possible—tall grass being the perfect cover. They patiently stalk their victims by creeping up on them, waiting for an opportunity. After Jesus' interactions with Satan, the Bible notes, "When the devil had finished all this tempting, he left him until an opportune time" (Luke 4:13). Timely surprise attacks give Satan a distinct advantage.

Lions are also known to get a herd moving in order to spot the weaker, younger, or slower members. On the run, they single out the vulnerable—those that become isolated from the herd or cannot keep up. Using their greater speed (up to 65 mph), size (up to 450 pounds), superior night vision, smell and hearing to pounce, they then use their massive jaws to lock onto the victim's neck, crushing its windpipe for a suffocating death. A lion's advantages are ones not easily overcome; we cannot outrun, outmuscle or hide from them. Far more, Satan can initiate natural disasters, cause personal accidents and disease and communicate in our inmost thoughts, to name a few of his advantages. Reread the first chapters of Job if this level of power surprises you.

In my own Christian life of twenty-five years, the most intense spiritual battles I faced were during an eight-month period as I was studying the Bible prior to my conversion. In retrospect, Satan clearly noted my weak spiritual condition and pounced. I was vulnerable. Was it coincidence that an ex-girlfriend appeared (one I admired for her Christian devotion) and pointedly tried to undermine my faith by bringing in a Bible expert to question my doctrine and church leaders? Was it coincidence that my company announced an abrupt closure of my regional office a few weeks after I was baptized? I could transfer to anywhere in the country, only I could not remain in my hometown, the fertile ground of my closest Christian friends and mentors. These were attacks meant to crush my new life in Christ.

Fortunately, God provides all of us with many spiritual weapons. In Ephesians 6:10-18, the Apostle Paul compares God's arms for us with those of a Roman soldier. We have divine weapons to fight the invisible and powerful spiritual forces pitted against us: 1) the Holy Spirit and his *Word* expose Satan's lies and express God's promises just as a sword inflicts pain on an enemy; 2) our own striving to be *personally righteous* is just as a Roman's breastplate guards his beating heart; 3) our mindset and *readiness* for the spiritual warfare ahead of us are as if our feet are ready to move quickly when necessary; 4) our quest to live with God forever in heaven compares to a helmet that protects a soldier's mind and senses; 5) our faith to see the schemes directed against us and expose them for what they are can be represented as shields that deflect flaming arrows meant to destroy us; and finally, 6) our prayers which mobilize godly forces to fight for us in the spiritual realms are offensive weapons we wield against our foe. The power of prayer cannot be underestimated.

It was through intense prayers during my early months as a Christian that I believe God provided the answers I needed and deepened my faith. It was as if I *saw* God as He spoke to me. Empowered by a deeply penetrating scripture (Matthew 19:29), I decided not to relocate, despite risking my promising career. By doing so, I firmly established that my spiritual life was now preeminent in my life. Within a few weeks, God provided me an easier job within my company that paid more money and enhanced my career. Simply, God blessed my decision.

How naïve I was long ago in doubting that Satan was real. How much I've learned about the invisible forces of evil in the heavenly realms. Yet, how vulnerable I realize I remain. My quest for spiritual learning is a lifetime pursuit. Undoubtedly, God is there to train me and fight for me in this spiritual war. I am convinced we must "fix our eyes not on what is seen, but on what is unseen. For what is seen is temporary, but what is unseen is eternal" (II Corinthians 4:18). So many are defenseless victims, unaware they're in a war they cannot see—just as I was.

...and you, how ready are you?

SPIRITUAL WARFARE: There's a Target on Your Back

Stuff to Talk Through With a Friend
* What would you see if you could see the spiritual world?
* What spiritual armor do you use on a regular basis to protect your spiritual life? What spiritual armor does God provide that you are not used to utilizing regularly?
* What are the tried and true schemes Satan has used to lead you to sin? For example:
  - money troubles/fears/allure
  - issues with sexual purity
  - marriage/family/personal conflicts
  - insecurities (job, relationships)
  - health problems
  - unfulfilling career/job
  - hopelessness/lack of motivation
  - overeating/addictive behaviors
  - false gods of material/career success

Things to Do If You Want to Grow
* A lack of forgiveness toward others is a common scheme of Satan's to twist another's unrighteous act toward you into your own unrighteous response. Be proactive by deciding to work through any lingering hurts now until your forgiveness toward them is complete. Ask for help from a mature Christian or counselor, if needed.
* Be sure to forge several friendships with whom you can confess and be open about any area of your life. Your humility and honesty are lights that help God disarm Satan's dark victories in your life. Commit yourselves to each other for this purpose.

SPIRITUAL WARFARE:
There's a Target on Your Back cont...

References for Further Bible Study

* Isaiah 14:12-15
  Satan's sin against God
* Ezekiel 28:12-19
  God's original creation of Satan and his sin and fall
* Daniel 10
  God's angel explains the delay to answering Daniel's prayer
* Job 1 and 2
  Satan and God's interaction as to what would befall Job
* John 8:42-47
  Jesus describing the Pharisees as being led by Satan
* Luke 4:1-13
  Jesus overcoming his own temptations by Satan
* Luke 22:31-34
  Satan's request to sift Peter as wheat and Jesus' commitment to pray for him

Additional Resources

The Lion Never Sleeps by Mike Taliaferro
Seeing the Unseen: Preparing Yourself for Spiritual Warfare by Joe Beam
This Present Darkness and Piercing the Darkness by Frank E. Peretti
The Complete Works of E.M. Bounds on Prayer
The Pineapple Story Audio CDs and The Snake Story DVD by Otto Koning
The Killer Within by Mike Taliaferro

For additional resources or to join our online community, go to:
http://fieldguide.faith21.org

21

Financial Stewardship
Whose Money Is It Anyway?

> *For the love of money is a root of all kinds of evil.*
> *Some people, eager for money, have wandered from the*
> *faith and pierced themselves with many griefs.*
> I Timothy 6:10

A common biblical misquote says that money is the root of evil. Rather, it is the LOVE of money, the thirst and desire for it, which produces all kinds of evil. There are many examples of righteous, wealthy people in the Bible. Among them are Abraham, David, Job, the Queen of Sheba and Joanna, just to name a few. In fact, personal wealth was seen as a blessing from God (Ecclesiastes 5:19-20). Having money does not necessarily mean that you love it. Wealthy philanthropists, who give away millions of dollars every year, don't seem to love money. At the same time, poor people can almost worship it!

Crimes from the heinous to the bizarre to the downright stupid have been committed over the love of money. The Bible calls this "ill-gotten gain" (Proverbs 10:2). Achan (Joshua 7:18-24), Ananias and Sapphira (Acts 5:1-10) and Judas (Matthew 27:1-5) loved money so much that they died because of it. All of these examples show us that money or being rich is not the real issue, for God gives us the power to create wealth (Deuteronomy 8:18). However, if we're enslaved by money or abuse it, it becomes sin before God. We must master our money, rather than being mastered by it (Genesis 4:7). The more money we have, the harder it becomes to master it. It could even hinder us from making it to Heaven, as Jesus indicated in Luke 18:25. Thankfully, the Bible is packed with wise counsel for our financial life!

God teaches us a completely new order of things, which is usually opposite of the world's standard. Money is no exception. Most of us don't have a money problem; we have a money management problem. The main cause of financial pressure comes from not understanding how to properly manage our money. It doesn't really matter how much we make. In fact, a person earning $20,000 per year who has learned to manage his or her money can be more financially independent than someone who earns $100,000 annually but hasn't learned fiscal management!

There are two main differences between how we often manage our money and the way God wants us to do it. The world's way:
1. Enjoy
2. Hopefully save
3. Maybe pay debts
4. Perhaps give to charity (and let everyone know!)
5. Avoid bill collectors, thinking they'll go away
6. If nothing else works, possibly make a plan

God's way:
1. Dedicate it all to him
2. Plan
3. Give

4. Save
5. Repay
6. Enjoy

Financial freedom isn't determined by our salary, but in how we spend what we have. By following the Bible's teachings on finances, we can relieve and prevent a great deal of stress in this area. Below is a brief overview of God's financial plan:

DEDICATE: Give to God first (Proverbs 3:9; I Corinthians 16:2).

PLAN: Live on less than you make (Proverbs 13:7). This is how to create emergency funds (eating out is not an emergency). Avoid borrowing money (Proverbs 22:7).

GIVE: God blesses generous people (Proverbs 11:24-25). He loves it when we enjoy giving (II Corinthians 9:7).

SAVE: The wise understand how to plan and save (Proverbs 21:20). The key is to be consistent!

PAY DEBTS: Take ownership of your debts and pay them on time (Romans 13:7-8). We can't expect to be trusted if we don't keep our word (II Corinthians 1:17). This includes ongoing bills like rent/mortgage and utilities. Here are some steps to become debt free:

1. Pray
2. List all of your debts beside everything you own
3. Establish a budget and a payment schedule
4. STICK to your budget and payment schedule!
5. Change your lifestyle to curb costs
6. Seek additional income through a part-time job
7. Don't give up!

> *Note: If you owe money to an individual, you must repay that debt before anything else, including giving to God. It would not be right to give or save what is not yours. However, debt to a financial institution is a business where the lender is making money off of the interest you pay, and so is unconcerned if you repay it slowly. Just make sure to stick to the payment schedule or even better, pay it off faster than required.*

ENJOY! God richly gives us all things for our enjoyment (I Timothy 6:17). When we enjoy what God has given, we bring him glory (Ecclesiastes 5:18-20).

For true financial success, we must follow the advice of Jesus, our Lord and ultimate financial advisor. He states in Matthew 6:21 that "where your treasure is, there your heart will be also." Our heart is always attached to our investment. Is our greatest investment in our bank account, or in the things of God? We can either deposit in our earthly life or make eternal deposits in Heaven. Financial saving is prudent (Luke 19:23), but we must make sure that nothing ever hinders our relationship with God. His way of acquiring, saving and spending money is very different to what we're accustomed, but it is the sure way to financial freedom. It is a matter of attitude and motive. We cannot LOVE both God and money (Matthew 6:24). When we follow God's advice, we have the satisfaction of knowing that we are living according to his amazing plan for our lives.

FINANCIAL STEWARDSHIP: Whose Money Is It Anyway?

Stuff to Talk Through With a Friend
* What struggles do you have in the area of finances?
* Have you shared your financial struggles with trusted friends?
* How do you feel about God owning everything and you owning nothing?
* Are you open and unified with your spouse regarding financial matters?
* How much debt are you in today?
* Are you driven by greed of any kind?

Things to Do If You Want to Grow
* Decide to develop a debt-free mindset.
* Seek advice and start a plan to pay off all of your debts.
* Look for ways to refresh others with what God has given you.
* Live on less for one day, then for one week, then for one month, then all the time. Keep track of how much money you save by doing this.

References for Further Bible Study
Psalm 24:1 • Proverbs 14:23 • Haggai 2:8 • Matthew 6 (entire chapter) • Luke 14:28-30 • Acts 8 (entire chapter) • I Corinthians 4:7 • II Corinthians 9:7

Additional Resources
Crown Financial Ministries www.crown.org
Books include:
- Managing Our Finances God's Way Study Guide
- Debt and Bankruptcy
- Investing and Insurance
- Spending Plan Solutions
- Work and Business
- Giving and Generosity
- Money Life Basics Complete Series
- Business by the Book

For additional resources or to join our online community, go to:
http://fieldguide.faith21.org

22

Generosity

It Is Better to Give Than to Receive

> *"For God so loved the world that he gave his one and only Son, that whoever believes in him shall not perish but have eternal life."*
> John 3:16

When considering the topic of giving, we first need to see and really understand that God is a giving God. Throughout scripture, God is always giving towards us: forgiveness, grace, compassion, mercy, blessings, protection, guidance, advice...Most importantly, we must never forget that he gave his Son to die for us.

Before we begin, we must be clear on one thing. This chapter focuses on giving monetarily, but giving money is not the only way to give. Other ways in which we can give back to God and help his church are all around us. For example, you can help with the children's program, administration, set up and tear down, and in many, many other ways. Ask someone to give you information about signing up for one of the ministries in your church. Giving is a matter of the heart more than a matter of the bank account. Money is the easy way to give, but it should not be the only way we give.

One of the first obstacles that you will encounter in your Christian walk is the idea that "the church" will ask you to give money. People might tell you that it is a scam when you are asked to give even a small percent of what you make. Some people will even tell you that giving a percentage of what you make is not required at all because Jesus never taught it. They forget that Jesus did say, "Then give to Caesar what is Caesar's, and to God what is God's" (Luke 20:25).

The truth is that, yes, most churches today will ask you to set aside a percentage of your wages, to be more specific, 10%, to give towards the needs of the church. The tithe, or 10%, is based on the Old Testament commandment for God's people to give 10% of everything they earned back to God (Leviticus 27:30; Malachi 3:10). The New Testament, written to you and me, is very clear on this issue of giving. Paul, in his second letter to the Corinthians, reminds us that we must give according to the needs (II Corinthians 8:14). He says that our giving should be according to what we have, or a percentage (II Corinthians 8:11-12). Most importantly, we should not be giving out of guilt or because we think we have to, but rather we must give cheerfully, from the heart (II Corinthians 9:7). As a Christian, you have the liberty to decide what percentage you can give cheerfully. The biblical principle of 10% has proven over the years to be the ideal amount in order to keep the church growing, and so it is still the standard today. When we consider that everything belongs to God anyway (Deuteronomy 10:14), giving a set percentage back to him becomes an easier choice.

When I first learned about tithing, I was surprised and didn't know what to think. However, when I looked deeper into it, I began to get excited. I had the privilege of working with God to keep his church alive and moving on this earth! After that, I truly looked forward to being a part of something bigger than my own life. If you are concerned about what the church is doing with the money, as I was, be open and tell someone about your concerns. Remember that you are not the first one to feel this way. Ask about it, study it out and get comfortable with it.

In addition to giving to support the regular needs of the church, the Bible also talks about special offerings (Deuteronomy 12:6; Malachi 3:8). These offerings are usually monetary gifts that we give to the church when special situations arise. For example, someone in the church may need help due to an overwhelming financial situation, money may be needed for missions, a natural disaster or equipment breakdown. You get the idea.

Funding missions in foreign lands is a very special opportunity to give. From the comfort of our own homes, we can actually help other people become Christians by giving a little more for missions or by helping someone who needs food and shelter. The needs are always there and God gives us an opportunity to give a little extra when we see the need. Keep in mind that these offerings should be in addition to what we give on a regular basis, not a part of it. Our regular giving, or tithe, is helping the church to function, while the special offerings are for helping others to live or to become Christians. In one of his letters, Paul talks about the Philippian church and their willingness to give special offerings. Paul was so grateful for them because they were filling a desperate need (Philippians 4:15). We need to follow their example in this area; Paul could be writing us the same letter today.

What a friend of mine told me has helped me be generous over the years. He said that our money only has the value that we give it. Say, for instance, you have $5 dollars and you spend it on a cup of coffee. You just decided that your $5 dollars were worth a cup of coffee. On the other hand, if you gave that money to a hungry child so he could get a meal, you just gave it a total different value. Which $5 dollars is worth more?

Obviously, sometimes it is easier to give than other times. When times are great, when the economy is doing good and we have a good job, we can, for the most part, give our tithe and offerings and sometimes not even think about it. On the other hand, if the economy is bad and our job is not the best, then tithing becomes a much more difficult challenge. However, we can do it if we trust in God's provision.

God has richly blessed my family in the last few years, more so than I could have ever imagined. I would love for you to experience the blessings that I have experienced through this privilege of giving.

GENEROSITY:
It Is Better to Give Than to Receive

Stuff to Talk Through With a Friend
* What type of comments are your relatives, friends and co-workers making as far as tithing goes?
* What are you learning, and how are you growing through those comments?
* Do you expect your giving and offering to be easy or hard? Why?
* How does this expectation affect your outlook on giving to the church?
* How does knowing you are not alone in your struggles make you feel?
* Do you expect to support or be a part of a ministry? Which one?

Things to Do If You Want to Grow
* Stop complaining about your money problems and start thanking God on a daily basis for the things he has already given you.
* Encourage a brother or sister who is going through a hard time.
* Listen to them, and, if they are open to it, share with them what you have learned.
* Ask for ways that you might be able to help the church by becoming a part of a ministry.
* Choose to do something definite to help.
* Read all the complete chapters suggested in this guide.

References for Further Bible Study
Leviticus 27 • Numbers 18 • Deuteronomy 12, 14 • Malachi 3 • Matthew 6:1-4 • Luke 20 • Philippians 4

Additional Resources
The Grace of Giving: A Biblical Study of Christian Stewardship by Edwin L., Jr. Frizen and Stephen F. Olford

Money Life Basics—Giving & Generosity and *Faith & Money: A Nontraditional Student Workbook* by Crown Financial Ministries (www.crown.org)

The Power of Gratitude by Gordon Ferguson

For additional resources or to join our online community, go to:
http://fieldguide.faith21.org

23

Living Sacrifice
Giving up Everything for Jesus

> So here's what I want you to do, God helping you: Take your everyday, ordinary life—your sleeping, eating, going-to-work, and walking-around life—and place it before God as an offering.
> Romans 12:1-2 (The Message)

The Christian life is not about trying to live your life within the rules. It also isn't about being good enough nor doing enough work for God to be pleased with you. The Christian life is about climbing up on the altar and laying yourself down as a sacrifice to God. You must be willing to sacrifice all of you, at any time, like Paul who asserts, "I have been crucified with Christ and I no longer live, but Christ lives in me…" (Galatians 2:20). In giving up your own life, you will discover a life within just waiting to flower outward. Jesus wants to take your sacrifice, and in return, give you life to the full.

When I became a Christian at age 19, I didn't have much to give God, as far as money goes. Even so, I was excited to have a new relationship with God and I wanted to express it somehow. I did things like give up eating food, especially food I liked. Sweet things, for instance, were a part of all my meals.

So, one time I went to the refrigerator and took out a delicious, cool, creamy pudding. Instead of eating it, I opened it and dumped it in the trash while saying "this is for *you* God." It was between me and God, and though my sacrificial pudding did not change the world (for the better, anyway), it taught me how to give up something that I really desired for God. Through the years, I have done a lot of things with this same sacrificial heart. Some sacrifices were big and very painful and some sacrifices were little and seemingly insignificant.

God sees all our little pudding sacrifices and at times may be just as pleased with them as he is with the big ones. Our goal as Christians is to offer every part of our lives, every moment, every action, our entire being to God (Mark 12:30). The more grateful and *in touch* we are with what God did and does for us, the more we will want to offer ourselves as living sacrifices to him. To whom much has been given, much is expected (Luke 12:48). How much has God given you?

Many of us have been inspired by sacrificial people in our lives. Moms, for instance, are usually the most sacrificial creatures among us, and mine is no exception. She is an amazing woman who has run herself into the ground in order to give her seven kids, and over 50 foster children, the best that she can. All her kids have new shoes, but she has holes in the bottom of hers.

The Bible is also full of examples of people who sacrificed. At one point in King David's story, he was instructed to offer a sacrifice to God from a particular location. The owner of that land, Araunah, offered to give it to him free of charge. David's response shows us his attitude towards sacrifice to God: "But the king replied to Araunah, "No, I insist on paying you for it. I will not sacrifice to the LORD my God burnt offerings that cost me nothing." So David bought the threshing floor and the oxen and paid fifty shekels of silver for them" (II Samuel 24:24).

Another example of a sacrificial life is Queen Esther in the Old Testament. She had everything she could ever want and would have been foolish to give it all up. However, when it came time to decide between her own safety and that of her people, she decided: "Go, gather together all the Jews who are in Susa, and fast for me. Do not eat or drink for three days, night or day. I and my maids will fast as you do. When this is done, I will go to the king, even though it is against the law. And if I perish, I perish" (Esther 4:16). Esther's whole story is amazing. At first, she was afraid for her life, but she decided to sacrifice herself for her people; even it meant her life.

During the process where I made the decision to give my life completely to God, I remember thinking that there was no other person in history that I wanted to be like more than Jesus. There were a lot of people that inspired me, but I realized that Jesus had all the qualities of these great men and women—and more. However, the most inspiring thing about Jesus, the one thing that made me want to follow him, was that he sacrificed his life for me!

Sacrifice is an amazingly powerful force. Bad is made good, the seemingly impossible is achieved, hearts are moved, circumstances are changed, families are unified, people are fed, lives are saved and dreams are fulfilled. The following anonymous poem describes what sacrifice looks like:

> *When you are forgotten, neglected, or purposely set at naught, and you don't sting or hurt with the oversight, but your heart is happy being counted worthy to suffer for Christ;*
> *That is dying to self.*
>
> *When your good is evil spoken of, when your wishes are crossed,*

your advice disregarded, your opinion ridiculed, and you refuse to let anger rise in your heart or even defend yourself, but take it all in patient, loving silence;
That is dying to self.

When you lovingly and patiently bear any disorder, any irregularity, any annoyance; when you can stand face to face with waste, folly, extravagance, spiritual insensibility, and endure it as Jesus did;
That is dying to self.

When you are content with any food, and offering, any raiment, any climate, any society, any solitude, any interruption by the will of God;
That is dying to self.

When you never care to refer to yourself in conversation or record your own good works or itch after commendation, when you can truly love to be unknown;
That is dying to self.

When you can see your brother prosper and have his needs met, and can honestly rejoice with him in spirit and feel no envy, nor question God, while your own needs are far greater and you are in desperate circumstances;
That is dying to self.

When you can receive correction and reproof from one of less stature than yourself and can humbly submit, inwardly as well as outwardly, finding no rebellion or resentment rising up within your heart;
That is dying to self.

LIVING SACRIFICE:
Giving up Everything for Jesus

Stuff to Talk Through With a Friend
* What can you sacrifice for God today?
* What sacrifice could you give to God that would challenge and inspire you?
* What makes an acceptable sacrifice to God?
* Is there anything in your life that you would not be able to sacrifice?

Things to Do If You Want to Grow
* Make a list of all the ways God has given to you. Be detailed.
* Practice sacrificing to God! Only you know what a true sacrifice would be.

References for Further Bible Study
Psalm 51:17 • II Corinthians 4:6-12 • Ephesians 5:1-2
Hebrews 13:15-16 • I Peter 2:1-5

Additional Resources
The Cost of Discipleship by Dietrich Bonhoeffer
The Cost of Commitment by John White, Don Everts
Foxe's Book of Martyrs by John Foxe
End of the Spear DVD from FoxFaith
Anchored for Life by Douglas Jacoby

For additional resources or to join our online community, go to:
http://fieldguide.faith21.org

24

Pride

The Hidden Killer

> *When pride comes, then comes disgrace,
> but with humility comes wisdom.*
> **Proverbs 11:2**

There is no soft way to say this: if not dealt with, your pride will kill you. You need to be fully aware that pride is one of the greatest threats to your relationship with God and that the key to fending off this threat is found nowhere else but in the humility of Jesus Christ. I know this not only from the Word of God, but also through my own experience. My experience has been a 13-year, knock-down, drag-out, bloody brawl with my own pride that has left me bruised, frustrated and somewhat embarrassed. The moment I relax in the belief that I've made some headway toward humility, I find my pride exposed all over again. Please know that this isn't a directive coming from a naturally humble man, but a warning to avoid the pitfalls I have fallen into.

My path to pride started with two decisions. One was conscious and the other subconscious.

I remember the very moment I made my first decision. The

place was Orange County, California. The time was my first day of high school, in late summer 1984. Until then, I had been the kid that nobody noticed, fading into the background without any impact, influence or perceived value. We had moved to a new school district, and since I was entirely unknown to everyone there, I decided that it was the time to grasp for something more. I decided to reinvent myself; I thought, "I will assume a sense of confidence, value, importance…I will be the one to be noticed…I will be the one with influence." I never expected it to work, but it did. That success firmly convinced me that if I just assume that "I'm the man," then other people will assume it too.

As life went on, I noticed people around me making bad decisions that often had negative results. I compared myself to them and assumed that since I was being more careful to avoid such bad choices, I must have better judgment. I was, in effect, making a subconscious decision to trust my thoughts and ideas above anyone else's.

That is my back-story…my experience. You have your own. Regardless of how pride has crept into your life, it is probably a more serious issue than you may be willing to accept. Don't take my word on the matter; look at what God's word says (Proverbs 15:25, 16:5; Leviticus 26:19; Isaiah 2:11; Jeremiah 13:17).

Why does God hold such special hatred towards pride? Aren't there other sins that are equally, if not more, destructive to humankind? Hatred…Lust…Greed…all these have wreaked so much destruction in the world! Surely they are worse than a harmless, internal attitude of pride.

First of all, we need not compare sins. All sin, big or small, is important to deal with (Romans 3:23). The immediate earthly impact is what we are addressing. Each sin affects us differently in our daily lives. Hatred brings violence, lust brings infidelity, greed brings discontentment, and so on. To understand God's special aversion to pride, we must ask ourselves the deeper questions: what is pride and what does it bring?

Pride is defined as a high or inordinate opinion of one's own dignity, importance, merit or superiority. In other words, it is the idolizing, satiating, protecting and glorification of SELF. In the simplest terms, pride is SELF-FOCUS.

So what does it bring? The answer is...SIN ITSELF!

I Timothy 6:10 says that greed is a root of all kinds of evil, but pride takes things a step further. While the Bible does not explicitly teach it, I have a strong suspicion that pride is the root of all sin. Think about the motivating factors behind the sinful acts committed by mankind: seeing what others have and wanting it for yourself: envy. Anger because things are not working out in your favor: wrath. Satisfying your sexual desire outside of marriage: lust. We could go on with gluttony, greed, sloth, vanity...When you consider the cause of every sin committed, you will find a person focused on himself. Our desires, needs, feelings, fears, self-esteem and general preservation of self prove ultimately important to us. As a result, we choose self over God and other people most of the time, often without realizing it. Pride, by its very nature, conceals itself from its host. It masks itself in the guise of intuition, common sense and the truth of our feelings. What we can clearly see as pride in another is hidden from our view of ourselves.

How do we as people become so self-focused? Some call it survival of the fittest, self-preservation, or just the natural isolation of the human soul. But in reality, it is simply our sinful nature running its course throughout human history. The reason why God holds special hatred for pride is because it is the cause of the world's suffering. Each of us must ask ourselves, "How am I contributing to this pandemic?"

Before becoming a Christian, I never questioned the spirituality of my decisions. My pride gave me the fulfillment in life that I desired, at least until my man-made peace of mind came to a screeching halt. When life came crashing down, I was, by the grace of God, given a chance to become a true disciple of Jesus Christ. Only then did I realize that the attitude that served me so well in the kingdom of men had become my greatest weaknesses in the kingdom of God. Over the past 13 years, I have struggled to find confidence in God rather than myself, to trust God's decisions over my own, to seek counsel with trust and respect, and ultimately, to find value in the righteousness that comes from God instead of comparing myself to others.

What we all need is something bigger, stronger and of greater value than ourselves. That is where the meekness of Christ comes in. At first glance, it seems that, if we embrace meekness, we will disappear into the background. We will lose value. To become nothing seems to be a pathway towards emptiness, and our nature cries out against it. Maybe that's the point. If our nature is the cause of so much sin, then we need to empty ourselves of that nature. Nothingness becomes the antidote. Becoming nothing was the example Jesus lived out for us (Matthew 11:29; Philippians 2:8; Psalm 25:9, 37:11, 149:4).

PRIDE: The Hidden Killer

Stuff to Talk Through With a Friend
* Do I often direct a conversation toward my opinion, ideas or experiences?
* Do I seek advice before making important decisions?
* Am I dismissive of others?
* Do I easily admit when I'm wrong?
* Do I often interrupt other people in mid-sentence?

Things to Do If You Want to Grow
* Start a Pride Journal (write down your prideful thoughts, motivations and actions).
* Periodically ask friends and family when and how they see pride in you.
* Never assume you have finally achieved humility.

References for Further Bible Study
* The story of King Uzziah—II Chronicles 26
* All of Philippians 2

Additional Resources
The Prideful Soul's Guide to Humility by Thomas Jones and Michael Fontenot
Humility by Andrew Murray

For additional resources or to join our online community, go to:
http://fieldguide.faith21.org

25

Deep Healing
God Longs to Heal Your Heart

> "He has sent me to bind up the brokenhearted, ...to comfort all who mourn, ...and provide for those who grieve in Zion—to bestow on them a crown of beauty instead of ashes, the oil of gladness instead of mourning, and a garment of praise instead of a spirit of despair."
> Isaiah 61:1-3

We are the brokenhearted. Our brokenness may be caused by our sin, other people's sin or by all kinds of loss: death, divorce, abuse, romantic heartbreak, financial and health issues, just to name a few. The symptoms of a broken heart are many: isolation, being "out of the moment," lack of energy, closing our hearts down, "protecting" ourselves by not loving again and hiding true feelings for fear of being judged. The grief caused by these losses can have tragic consequences if not dealt with in the right way. Losing a loved one, for example, is one of the most common reasons people turn their backs on God. All of us are broken in some way, and if we ever want to truly experience happiness, we must heal completely.

The first step to healing is dealing correctly with the pain caused by our losses. Grief is a normal, natural response to loss. It is emotional, not intellectual. This is why intellectual approaches to grief don't work. Well-meaning but misinformed people try to help with comments like "don't feel bad," "get over it" or "be strong" that just shut us down.

Our culture also feeds us myths like "time heals all wounds," "keep busy" or "replace the loss." These can only serve as obstacles to healing. Even statements like "God will never give you more than you can handle," while intellectually true (I Corinthians 10:13), are not emotionally helpful and can direct our anger toward God (Lamentations 3:33). Simply put, you cannot heal the heart with the head; you must deal with the heart directly.

Turning to short-term relief through alcohol, drugs, sex, shopping, food or even busyness to deal with our grief will not work either. Not only do these behaviors carry with them their own consequences, they don't address the root issue. Rather than a temporary distraction or escape from our pain, God wants to heal us at our core for lasting, permanent relief.

So where do we turn when our best efforts, the world's wisdom and well-meaning friends can't help us? The Bible reassures us that "The Lord is close to the brokenhearted and saves those who are crushed in spirit...He heals the brokenhearted and binds up their wounds" (Psalm 34:18, 147:3). God's heart of love for us far exceeds anything we have experienced elsewhere. He is the Father of compassion and the God of all comfort (II Corinthians 1:3). This is why such a large part of Jesus' ministry was dedicated to healing people. God not only can help us, he longs to (Isaiah 30:18-19).

Years ago, a dear friend of mine was in despair. She told me God needed to help her that day or she would leave him. She had been sexually and emotionally abused in her youth and had learned to "act healed" and grieve alone. All that buried pain was eating away at her and she was ready to explode. Thankfully, God did begin healing her that same day. He led her to a Grief Recovery class where she was able to learn practical tools to help with her losses. She is now happily married, a mom and an active part of her church. Satan tried to take her out when she was young, but because of her courage and willingness to deal with her pain, God has healed her heart and transformed her life.

We must step out on faith that God can, and will, heal us. We also need to be urgent because unresolved grief is an easy target for Satan to attack and gain a foothold in our hearts. Our first step is to take responsibility and be proactive in our own recovery (John 5:6-8).

How? We must stop judging others, or ourselves, and stop comparing or minimizing our pain (Luke 6:37). Only when we are real, open and honest enough to bring things into the light (James 5:16; I John 1:9) will we have the clarity necessary to see the next required action. We may need to repent of sin, confront someone, apologize or forgive. If we are struggling with a physical illness, mental disorder or issues beyond the depth of those in our lives, we may need to seek professional help.

The majority of our brokenness occurs within relationships. Healing is attainable by discovering and completing all our undelivered communications: apologies, forgiveness and other significant emotional statements. In other words, if you have sinned against someone or hurt them in any way, apologize. If someone has sinned against you or hurt you (or someone you love) in any way, forgive them. If this is difficult, please understand that forgiveness is not the same as condoning. Forgiveness will set you free from the pain of an offense against you and has little to do with the other person.

The shortest sentence in the Bible is just two words: "Jesus wept" (John 11:35). At the grave of his friend Lazarus, Jesus felt the pain of those around him and was moved to tears. Likewise, God feels our pain and wants to heal us. We need to imitate Jesus' example in the grieving process and not be afraid to face and express our pain so that we too can be set free. "Then your light will break forth like the dawn, and your healing will quickly appear; then your righteousness will go before you, and the glory of the LORD will be your rear guard" (Isaiah 58:8).

Seeking Professional Help

There are those who think we shouldn't need anything other than the Bible to help us. The Bible does thoroughly equip us for every good work (II Timothy 3:17); however, it is sometimes necessary to use outside resources to learn how to apply biblical principles. God has allowed for the development of many fields of expertise to assist us. Treat your needs in the emotional arena in the same way you would treat cancer: go to God in prayer *first*, then see a specialist and trust God will use them to heal you. With therapy, make every effort to go to a Bible-based counselor or therapist. Stay open with Christians in your life and pray for discernment through the entire process. Through it all, keep in mind that God is the one who heals you, not a person or program—they are just the tools he is using (Acts 3:16). Give him gratitude and glory for all victories (Jeremiah 17:14).

DEEP HEALING:
God Longs to Heal Your Heart

Stuff to Talk Through With a Friend
* Do you believe that God can heal you (Romans 4:18-21; Mark 9:23-24)?
* Are you willing to do whatever it takes to be healed (John 5:6-8; II Corinthians 7:11)?
* Is there anything you have been holding onto from your past that you need to deal with or get free from? Bring it into the light through confession (James 5:16; I John 1:8-10).
* Do you struggle with any addictions (drugs, alcohol, sex, shopping, food, lying, etc.)? Seek help to repent (II Corinthians 7:8-11; Romans 2:4).
* Is there anyone in your life whom you need to apologize to (Proverbs 14:9)?
* Is there anyone in your life whom you need to forgive (Matthew 18:21-35)?

Things to Do If You Want to Grow
* Deal with any addictions.
* Enroll in a Grief Recovery program.
* Be open with brothers and sisters who have overcome the same challenges you are facing and imitate what they have done to conquer them (Hebrews 13:7).
* Is there someone in your life undergoing a struggle you have overcome? Share your experience with them and what helped you through it (II Corinthians 1:3-7). Keep in mind that what is helpful for one person may not always be helpful for another.

References for Further Bible Study
Isaiah 19:22, 57:18-19 • Jeremiah 33:6-9 • Matthew 4:23, 8:7, 8:28, 9:6, 10:8, 13:15, 17:14, 18:21-35 • Colossians 3:13

DEEP HEALING: God Longs to Heal Your Heart cont...

Additional Resources

Grief Recovery Institute (www.grief.net)

The Grief Recovery Handbook: The Action Program for Moving Beyond Death, Divorce, and Other Losses by John W. James and Russell Friedman

When Children Grieve: For Adults to Help Children Deal with Death, Divorce, Pet Loss, Moving, and Other Losses by John W. James, Russell Friedman, and Dr. Leslie Matthews

Moving On: Dump Your Relationship Baggage and Make Room for the Love of Your Life by Russell Friedman and John W. James

The Wounded Heart: Hope for Adult Victims of Childhood Sexual Abuse by Dan B Allender Ph.D.

From Bondage to Bonding: A Working Guide to Recovery from Codependency and Other Injuries of the Heart by Nancy J. Groom

This Doesn't Feel Like Love: Trusting God When Bad Things Happen by Roger and Marcia Lamb

Finding God: In Pain and Problems an Audio Series by Thomas Jones

A Grief Observed by C.S. Lewis

The Way of the Heart by G. Steve Kinnard

Walking the Way of the Heart by G. Steve Kinnard

For additional resources or to join our online community, go to:
http://fieldguide.faith21.org

CHRISTIAN CONUNDRUMS
Why Did Jesus Die?

Have you ever asked yourself *how* it is that Jesus' death saves you? *Why* is it that Jesus died so you can go to heaven? The Bible doesn't really say. Following are a few popular explanations:

Substitution Theory (Introduced in 1000 AD)

Mankind's sin deserves death (Romans 6:23). In order for God to be just, he needed to punish sinners to the full. Jesus offered himself to God as a substitution for all of mankind. When Jesus died on the cross, God poured out on him all of his wrath so that we do not have to suffer the punishment we deserve.

Moral Example Theory (Introduced in 1100 AD)

God's great love and kindness, shown through Jesus' death, are what softens man's heart so that he believes and changes for the better (Romans 2:4). God does not need any sacrifice in order to forgive sin. In fact, Jesus' death would not have been strictly necessary, except to show us God's amazing love.

Ransom Theory (Original Theory)

Jesus offered himself as a ransom (Mark 10:45) for us who had sinned and thus sold ourselves into Satan's domain. In a surprise move, Jesus triumphed over the Devil breaking out of Hell, freeing many captives and rising to life on the third day. Satan no longer has dominion over us, who are bought with Jesus' blood.

For God loved the world so much that he gave his only Son, so that everyone who believes in him should not be lost, but should have eternal life.
John 3:16 (J.B. Phillips)

26

Love
The Greatest Commandment

*The entire law is summed up in a single command:
"Love your neighbor as yourself."*
Galatians 5:14

From cover to cover, the Bible is filled with amazing stories. Exciting tales of adventure, intrigue, mystery, suspense and even terror fill its pages. Taken as a whole, a reader can see that the Bible is a tapestry whose patterns have been carefully woven through time with the sole purpose of showing the relationship between the Creator and creation. Of all the lessons which may be learned from reading God's word, love is the theme holding everything else together.

Karl Barth, one of the most important theologians of the 20th century, was once asked for the greatest theological thought which had ever come into his mind. After careful consideration, Barth replied, "Jesus loves me this I know, for the Bible tells me so." Whether Barth was serious in his answer or just being clever, his words are profound and true. John 3:16 says, "For God so loved the world that he gave his only Son, so that everyone who believes in him may not perish but may have eternal life." Jesus was sent to Earth in order that God's love might be demonstrated to us through his sacrifice and forgiveness. It is important to remember that this act of God's love is both a continuation and culmination of the innumerable times God has shown love towards humanity. We all believe this, at least intellectually. Why else would we have become Christians if we had any doubt of God's love for us? His love goes beyond the natural affection of a Creator towards his creation and has taken on a life of its own. God's purpose for humanity, the reason he created us, can be expressed in one single word—love.

Matthew 22:34-40 tells of a Pharisee who, in an attempt to test Jesus, asked which is the greatest commandment in the law. Jesus replied: "'Love the Lord your God with all your heart and with all your soul and with all your mind.' This is the first and greatest commandment. And the second is like it: 'Love your neighbor as yourself.' All the Law and the Prophets hang on these two commandments." What a powerful statement. Jesus reminded this expert in the Law that every act of religious obedience revolves around love for God and love for one another. Jesus goes a step further in John 13:34 when he gives the "new" command to "Love one another. As I have loved you, so you must love one another. By this all men will know that you are my disciples, if you love one another." Love for one another was a command which the religious leaders had either forgotten or forsaken. In Matthew 23:23, Jesus issues a stern rebuke to the teachers of the Law and the Pharisees who, in their zeal for religious obedience, gave their whole tithe while at the same time neglecting "the more important matters of the law—justice, mercy and faithfulness." The lack of justice, mercy and faith are symptoms of a heart that lacks love for God and God's people. Even the most cursory reading of the Bible, both Old and New Testaments, reveals the fact that most of God's discipline towards humanity comes because of a lack of love and respect for God and one another.

Several years ago, a good friend of mine died while saving his son's life. His death hit me pretty hard because we had fallen out of touch. I had only been able to chat with him when on occasion we would run into each other; and yet my friend is the example of love upon which I desire to pattern my walk as a Christian. The common consensus of the many people who showed up at his memorial service was that my friend was a man who lived a life of love and service. Family, both physical and spiritual, took top priority in his life. He was a good friend to everyone who knew him. He was a great husband to his wife, father to his children (as well as the children of many others) and brother in Christ to God's family.

At work, my friend was a true professional; a talented artist who did wonders in the film animation industry with an incredible list of credits to his name. The men and women he worked with saw the light in his life and honored his commitment and integrity even if they did not share his faith in God. My friend made it a habit to create a family atmosphere in whatever capacity he could serve whether at home, work, in his neighborhood or at church. He lived his life attempting to fulfill God's dream and purpose for him. My friend lived his life building family. He lived his life with love.

There are many things we will learn as we grow in our lives as Christians and as we search out God's purpose for our lives. We will teach, preach, lead and serve. We will help feed the poor, clothe the homeless, encourage the downtrodden and help bring the gospel to those who need it. We will do great things in our walk as a Christian. However, no matter what insightful things we may learn and great things we may do, we must keep in mind Paul's words in I Corinthians 13: "If I speak in the tongues of men and of angels, but have not love, I am only a resounding gong or a clanging cymbal. If I have the gift of prophecy and can fathom all mysteries and all knowledge, and if I have a faith that can move mountains, but have not love, I am nothing. If I give all I possess to the poor and surrender my body to the flames, but have not love, I gain nothing."

LOVE: The Greatest Commandment

Stuff to Talk Through With a Friend
* Do I agree with Karl Barth? Is the fact that Jesus loves me the most important thing I have learned as a Christian?
* What interferes with my ability to love others the same way Jesus loves me?
* How can I show the love of Christ to the people in my life?

Things to Do If You Want to Grow
* Are you like my friend? Commit to having the people you work with, go to school with or live with see you loving like Jesus loves.
* Find someone today who you think needs to be loved and do something loving for them. Tomorrow, try it again.

References for Further Bible Study
John 3:16 • Proverbs 3:3, 7:18 • Matthew 22:37-39 • Romans 12:10, 13:8-9

Additional Resources
Divine Romance by Gene Edwards
Love One Another: Becoming the Church Jesus Longs For by Gerald L Sittser

For additional resources or to join our online community, go to:
http://fieldguide.faith21.org

27

Born Identity
I Know Whose I Am

> *For it is by grace you have been saved, through faith—
> and this not from yourselves, it is the gift of God—not
> by works, so that no one can boast. For we are God's
> workmanship, created in Christ Jesus to do good works,
> which God prepared in advance for us to do.*
> Ephesians 2:8-10

Have you ever heard the idea that we tend to view God in the same way we view our own father? Our experience of God as our father is deeply rooted in our own experiences of fatherhood. Take a moment to think about your own childhood and what your overall experience of your father was. Did he support you, love you, and encourage you? Did he express his love for you just as you were, or did he control, manipulate, and criticize you? Maybe he just wasn't around, or if he was, maybe it didn't feel like it. Whatever your experience, look at your relationship with God as your father. Do you see any similarities?

Now consider that your view of God isn't entirely accurate.

Growing up had its challenges for me. My dad was not the most positive father, though I know he loved us in his own way and sacrificed and provided for us faithfully. He had a tendency to focus on the negative, including anything to do with my siblings or me, and would express those things freely. Life just looked that way for him, I guess.

I can still hear his voice repeating things to me like, "Why don't you try to be more like this friend of yours?" or "You should be like so-and-so..." When I got straight A's and one B+, he would comment first in disappointment at the B+. Then there were the performance-based praises that came only when I succeeded, or when I was better than my brothers or sisters at something. The compliments usually came with a comparison, whether it was the compliments aimed at me or just the comparisons.

Sometimes he would paint a vision of what I could be in his eyes (a prize-winning author, a renowned architect, a child prodigy), and I believed that when I attained that height of fame and glory, then he would be proud of me, then he would accept me.

I began to view my dad's love for me as conditional. He could only love me when I did something good, when I was the best—when I was perfect. And of course, being a child, I felt deeply that it was all my fault. I wasn't good enough. I had to do more, be better, excel beyond everyone else to stand out enough to deserve my father's love.

Of course, when I became a Christian, that's exactly what I believed about my relationship with God. Thankfully, that isn't true. God cares more about us than what we can do for him, "as if he needed anything" (Acts 17:25).

Then the question is, how does God really feel about us? Who are we to him?

First, we are God's masterpiece.

God saved you by his grace when you believed. And you can't take credit for this; it is a gift from God. Salvation is not a reward for the

good things we have done, so none of us can boast about it. For we are God's masterpiece. He has created us anew in Christ Jesus, so we can do the good things he planned for us long ago.
Ephesians 2:8-10 (New Living Translation)

This scripture says that he loves us apart from what we do for him, yet because of his love for us, he planned good things for us to do even before we chose him, even before we did something "right" in his eyes, before we "deserved" to be used. It is God accomplishing good things through us, not something we did ourselves (Philippians 2:13).

We'll never deserve what God gives us, by the way. No matter how many scriptures we've memorized, or friends we've introduced to God, or any other spiritual work we may want to wave in front of God's face and say, "See what I did? Love me now!"—we'll still be the same hopeless creatures he loved and knew he would need to die for to make clean and right before him.

Second, we are God's chosen. We belong to him (Ephesians 1:11-14). God chose us before we even knew how to be right with him. He loved us while we were still enemies sinning against him (Romans 5:8-10), so why do we think he is waiting for us to attain a certain level of spirituality before he can accept us?

We are God's children, his heirs (Romans 8:16-17). As his own flesh (or spirit) and blood, how could God reject us? When he redeemed us, he gave us the right to everything that is his. Like the prodigal son, even if we were to reject him and waste all that he's given us, he would still love us and take us back (Luke 15:11-32).

Understanding that we are unconditionally loved by God, we can seek to accomplish spiritual goals out of gratitude and joy, not out of a need to be accepted because of our accomplishments or skill.

Like our friendly neighborhood Spiderman learned, "With great power comes great responsibility." Now that we have been saved—now that we have been loved unconditionally and brought into God's wonderful family—what do we want to do? What does God want us to do?

To live as Jesus did (John 14:12). To love others as he loves us (John 15:12). To share out of the overflow of what he gives us (Philemon 6).

Freely we have been given to, now let's freely give (Matthew 10:8).

BORN IDENTITY: I Know Whose I Am

Stuff to Talk Through With a Friend
* How does my view of my own father affect my relationship with God?
* What does God want me to do in response to his love?
* What has my motivation for doing spiritual things been in the past?
* What does God want my motivation to be?
* What has God put on my heart to do for him?

Things to Do If You Want to Grow
* Talk to God about your misconceptions of him, and ask him to reveal himself more and more to you. Be very honest with him about how you've felt about his relationship with you. Ask him to open your heart to his true love.
* Make a list of spiritual goals that you want to accomplish for God. Pray each day for a week for God to make clear which goal you should focus on, and ask him for the right heart in pursuing the goal. Make it about God's glory, not your own. Pray for God to accomplish it through you.
* Share your goal with a spiritual partner, and tell them when you are aiming to accomplish your goal. Jesus set goals for himself (Luke 13:32).

References for Further Bible Study
Ephesians 1:4, 2:6, 2:13-15, 4:1, 4:24 • Colossians 3:10 • Titus 2:14

Additional Resources
Abba's Child by Brennan Manning
He Loves Me! Learning to Live in the Father's Affection by Wayne Jacobson
In the Grip of Grace by Max Lucado
If You Want to Walk on Water, You've Got to Get Out of the Boat by John Ortberg
The Shack by William P. Young

For additional resources or to join our online community, go to:
http://fieldguide.faith21.org

28

Sowing and Reaping
Pulling up the Roots

> *But the fruit of the Spirit is love, joy, peace, patience, kindness, goodness, faithfulness, gentleness and self-control. Against such things there is no law.*
> Galatians 5:22-23 (New Living Translation)

Botany, unless you are agriculturally inclined, probably ranks up there as one of the most mundane subjects. Yet the Bible frequently employs farming metaphors to describe evangelism (John 4:36), the Holy Spirit (Galatians 5:22-23), the consequences of our sins (Matthew 3:10) and numerous other matters of spiritual importance. These metaphors offer a great deal of insight into living in a way that honors God's design for our lives. To understand God's design, it is necessary to understand how fruit is produced—it all begins with the seed.

Whatever type of seed is planted in the soil will determine the kind of fruit the tree will bear. Every seed, if properly watered and protected, contains the potential to reproduce itself. The fruitfulness of the seed depends upon the quality of the soil in which it is planted. After the seed has been planted, the root system begins to develop and eventually sprouts germinate. Keep in mind that it is impossible for the tree to grow beyond what its root system can sustain. Once the tree begins to bear fruit, the fruit must be picked. If it is not picked, the fruit drops to the ground, dies, and may one day reproduce itself. After each harvest season, the branches need to be pruned. The process of pruning causes healthier and stronger growth and produces even more fruit the following season.

A farmer who intended to grow apples would never plant carrot seeds. Although this might seem elementary, how often have we looked at the "bad fruit" of our lives—depression, faithlessness, anxiety, worry, bitterness, lust, jealousy or greed—and concluded that we just need to manage our sin more effectively? On the contrary, Matthew 12:33 reminds us that we must do more than deal with the fruit: "Make a tree good and its fruit will be good, or make a tree bad and its fruit will be bad, for a tree is recognized by its fruit." God would *really* prefer we not attempt to manage our sins. Rather, he prefers that we do some weeding and pull the sins out by their roots. How do we usually respond when seed planted in the soil of our hearts grows roots deep enough to become a tree that bears fruit—fruit that is poisonous? Well, we might take out some shears and begin energetically pruning our overgrown and unmanageable branches (John 15:2). Does pruning the tree change the fruit? *Not at all*. What if we get really aggressive and hack the branches down to the trunk? *The fruit remains the same.* Remember, we reap what we sow (Galatians 6:7-10).

Seeds, like doubt, faithlessness and self-centeredness, can lead to root systems that are almost impossible to dig up on our own. For example, people growing up in a loveless, abusive situation might doubt God's love for them. This seed leads to a belief system that they must take care of themselves since nobody, including God, is going to. This root system may then lead to many different types of sin like worry or selfishness.

Pruning the branches bearing bad fruit will not bring lasting change. It can only bring temporary relief and mask the real problem.

To make matters worse, the branches always grow back—even bigger than before. After investing so much time and effort into pruning, we are usually left exhausted, discouraged or worse. If we have not relied on God (the Gardener) to do the pruning, the fruit will never change since we can only bear fruit according to the seed we have planted. In John 15:4, Jesus teaches that on our own we cannot bear good fruit, but must rely on him: "Remain in me, and I will remain in you. No branch can bear fruit by itself; it must remain in the vine. Neither can you bear fruit unless you remain in me."

Bad fruit in our lives does not always come from seeds planted by us. A bad seed can also develop roots when someone hurts our feelings or when we are sinned against. If we let that person's opinion of us dictate how we act or even feel about ourselves, then we form a subconscious agreement with the very thing that hurt us. Eventually, this type of agreement produces all kinds of poisoned fruit: faithlessness, using our outward appearance to gain acceptance, self-esteem issues, fearfulness, lack of trust, anxiety and the need to be in control. Ultimately, we may come to believe that we are not good enough to be children of God. In other words, our experiences (seeds) have developed agreements (root systems) which eventually bear bad fruit (faithlessness, etc.).

Our only hope lies in praying for God to reveal the underlying root system of the bad fruit in our lives (John 15:5). If we are willing to honestly examine our fruit, it becomes very easy to identify the seed that was planted (Matthew 7:16; I John 5:1-5). After the root system has been identified and uprooted, the bad seed must be replaced with the good seed of God's truth. God will do most of the work, but we have our part to play as well.

God promises that we can produce good fruit because, as Jesus reminds us, "You did not choose me, but I chose you and appointed you to go and bear fruit—fruit that will last. Then the Father will give you whatever you ask in my name" (John 15:16). Our part is to let him do the work and feed daily on his truth by spending time with him. If we determine that the root system of some of our sin comes from agreements we made when hurt by others, we are called to forgive (Romans 5:15-17). Understanding God's undying love for us, despite how we have sinned against him, motivates us to forgive others and embrace our true identity as his sons and daughters. As children of God, "...the law no longer holds you in its power, because you died to its power when you died with Christ on the cross. And now you are united with the one who was raised from the dead. As a result, you can produce good fruit, that is, good deeds for God" (Romans 7:4, NLT).

God never misses any roots, and he only plants excellent seed that produces the best fruit. He is the ultimate Gardener.

SOWING AND REAPING: Pulling up the Roots

Stuff to Talk Through With a Friend
* What "fruit" is on your tree?
* What composes your "root system?"
* What "weeds" do you need to uproot?

Things to Do If You Want to Grow
* Spend time reviewing your life. List the "fruit" that is on your tree and the "root systems" that support it.
* Find a scripture that shows how God views each of the "root systems."
* Pray through each and every agreement you have made after being hurt by others, and specifically ask God to break the agreements in Jesus' name.
* Spend time with God each day receiving the good seed of his truth found in the Bible.

References for Further Bible Study
Job 4:8 • Proverbs 11:18 • Hosea 10:12 • Romans 11:16-18 • Galatians 6:7-8 • Hebrews 12:15

Additional Resources
Changes That Heal: How to Understand the Past to Ensure a Healthier Future by Henry Cloud

29

Life to the Full
Where Is This Life We Are promised?

"I am the gate; whoever enters through me will be saved. He will come in and go out, and find pasture. The thief comes only to steal and kill and destroy; I have come that they may have life, and have it to the full."
John 10:9-10

Many Christians have asked the question, "Where is this life to the full that we've been promised?" In order to answer that question, we need to understand what Jesus meant by "life to the full" or "abundant life." Contrary to what we hear today, when Jesus spoke of "abundant" life, he was not referring to success, fame, material blessings and riches of this world. No, he was speaking of spiritual blessings; of eternal life. In this same chapter, Jesus tells the Jewish leaders that he is the door to eternal life and claims to be the Good Shepherd who has come to rescue us, to save us from death (Psalm 68:20). In another passage, Jesus claimed to be the Way, the Truth and the Life (John 14:6-7).

The Apostle Paul also speaks of this life in Christ throughout his letters to the churches. In Ephesians, he encourages and reassures the believers of the abundant life and blessings we have in Christ. He describes those blessings as a life full of forgiveness, grace and the greatest gift of all, the Holy Spirit (Ephesians 1:3-14). Note that these are three powerful blessings that we never had before Christ. With Christ, our lives no longer need be full of shame and regret; rather, they can be full of a living hope (I Peter 1:3-9). This hope does not disappoint us when we look for our fulfillment in God rather than in the things of this world (Romans 5:1-5).

When I consider my "life" before becoming one of Jesus' sheep, I quickly realize that it was all a façade, a big, fat lie. Everything I have pursued in this life has left me empty: drugs, sex, fame and fortune. I tried to fill the void in my life with people, pleasures and things; to live life to the full on my own terms. None of that held a candle to the life I found in Christ, or the overwhelming freedom I felt when I first dedicated my life to Jesus and was baptized. He gave me freedom from the shame and burden of my sins, and filled me with gratitude, joy and hope. The empty void in me was now indwelt by the fullness of God (Ephesians 3:14-20).

From the beginning, I understood I had to give up my old life (Colossians 3:5-10). So I did; I gave up everything for the incredible joy of knowing Christ. The hardest to give up were my friends and family, whom Satan was using to damage my faith and entice me to return to my sins. My reward has been great; not only do I have eternal life, but I have literally hundreds of close friends that have laid down their lives for me, as I have for them (Matthew 19:29; John 15:12-14). Not only that, having grown in my faith and beliefs, I am now able to influence my family and old friends for Christ. Over the years, they have seen a display of God's amazing power and love in my life as he continuously blesses and changes me.

The first definition of the abundant life that is promised by God is simple: the old life is crucified so that a new life can take its place. This new life is eternal, abundant, full and in Christ. It contains two components of life that truly make life worth living: love and purpose.

Love is the one thing we all truly desire (Proverb 19:22). The best example of love is, of course, Jesus, who exemplified God's eternal love for us (Isaiah 54:10) by giving up his very life. For sure, most of us have experienced love from our friends and family. But if we are honest, we must admit that their love has often failed us. We have sought to be satisfied and validated by people when it is only God who truly satisfies (Psalm 90:14). In him, we are complete, for his love endures forever. When we are feeling hurt, disappointed, insecure, disrespected or worthless, we can cry out to God to satisfy and sustain us with his love and validate us with his truth. I can testify that he faithfully gives me a peace and confidence that could only come from a loving God (Isaiah 32:17; John 14:26-27; II Corinthians 3:4-5).

What was the point of our old lives? Our way of living was merely passed on to us from our families and friends (I Peter 1:18-19); there was no true purpose in them. We may have wanted to be good people, have solid educations and work jobs to make us lots of money, but that is not a real purpose. Some of us may have longed to get married and have children, or even to be good humanitarians, save the Earth and stop starvation—all great things in themselves, but they will leave us empty if God is not the motivation of our hearts. On the other hand, as we live for God in everything, we will find that our life has an eternal purpose (Colossians 3:24). This purpose, according to scripture, is to love God and others (Matthew 22:36-40; Colossians 1:27). It is imperative that we understand our purpose and put it into practice; the world is waiting to see that we are truly disciples of Christ (II Corinthians 5:20; John

13:34). Love should be the core virtue of our Christian walk (Colossians 3:12-14; I Corinthians 13:13).

In summary, we are asked to die to our old life and promised that, in return, we will be raised with Christ and given the same life he had when he rose from the dead. This life has the earthly blessing of love from God and others in *his* family as well as a very real purpose for our lives. This life also has the blessing of an eternity with God, a gift beyond all comprehension. Let us go out and be about our purpose of loving others in the hope of giving them access to this life to the full.

LIFE TO THE FULL:
Where Is This Life We Are Promised?

Stuff to Talk Through With a Friend
* Do I feel like I experience life to the full?
* Is there any aspect of my old life that I am holding onto? What will it take to surrender it?

Things to Do If You Want to Grow
* Take a few minutes to write down key elements of your life prior to becoming a Christian. Use this list to remind yourself what your life used to be like.
* Ask a close Christian friend if they see life to the full when they look at you.
* Ask a close non-Christian friend how they see your life on a scale of 1 to 10: 1 being stressful; 10 being joyful.

References for Further Bible Study
John 1:4, 4:14, 14:6 • Philippians 4:7 • Psalm 23:6, 36:9

Additional Resources
God's Best Secret by Andrew Murray
The Fruitful Life: The Overflow of God's Love Through You by Jerry Bridges
Soul-ed Out by Gordon Ferguson

For additional resources or to join our online community, go to:
http://fieldguide.faith21.org

30

Finding Your Shape
Exploring Your Unique Purpose

> *For we are God's masterpiece. He has created us anew in Christ Jesus, so that we can do the good things he planned for us long ago.*
> **Ephesians 2:10 (NLT)**

What is God's will for my life? Now that you're a Christian, the answer seems simple: live a life that attracts others to Christ. But what is God's will for *your* unique life? *That* is probably the most important question anyone can ask. Even after becoming Christians, it still burns in our chests. Now the question is prodding us to discover how we should be spending our time each day and what special trajectory God has planned for the path of our new life. According to Ephesians 2:10, they are "good things" that God has had "planned for us" for quite a while. Does God offer any clues as to what those things might be, and do we get a say in any of it?

God created everyone and set the times and the exact places where we all would live, for one reason...so that we would seek him and have the best possible opportunity to find him (Acts 17:24-27). In the process of becoming a Christian, you discover that God's will is no longer a mystery, though you may not always understand it (Ephesians 1:9; Isaiah 59:2). Learning what God's will is serves as the key to our destiny! If God designed everything on earth with his reason and purpose in mind, that means we were created and designed for that exact same reason and purpose. In other words, we were uniquely created to give others in our lives the best possible opportunity to seek and find God! Have you ever thought of yourself in those terms?

Psalm 139:14-16 speaks of how we were "fearfully and wonderfully made" and tells us that God wove us together with all our days ordained for us before any came to be. We are not clones, we are masterpieces—works of art. Therefore, we need to think on that grandiose scale when deciding what we are to do with our time. Acts 17 states that God allows us to seek him and "perhaps reach out for him." *Perhaps?* This means that God is leaving it all up to you and me. He has set everything up in our favor, but we must make the decisions.

Can we be and do anything we want? No. But we can be everything God wants us to be, even if it isn't what we or others might expect. God has commissioned each individual item he created to accomplish very different things. The sun achieves one thing while trees accomplish another and still rain carries out another; yet they serve one purpose. And so it is with each of us.

There is no one else like you. That is why it is so important for you to discover *specifically* what God has you here to do. Without understanding that, you could easily decide to do things God never intended or designed you to do. If your gifts don't meet the role you play in life, you feel out of place and frustrated, you waste your talents, time and energy and you limit your results. On the other hand, have you ever met someone who loves what he does and obviously is doing exactly what he is supposed to be doing with his life? That is the person God wants you to be! However, he doesn't hand it to you immediately; your journey of actively seeking his will is important to develop character, and for others to see.

So, where do you start?

Start with your dreams. What do you hope for and dream of? Are there certain subjects, activities or circumstances that make your heart race when you think about them? This can give you clues as to what you should be doing to fully live in God's will.

With your dreams in focus, you must apply faith, which specifically is "being sure of what you hope for and certain of what you do not see" (Hebrews 11:1). God uses your hopes and dreams to get you to take action in life—for him. Use your dreams to figure out your daily activities. In his *Wild at Heart— Field Manual,* John Eldridge says:

> *"Your goal is to recover that adventure God wrote on your heart when He made you. Your deepest desires reveal your deepest calling, the adventure God has for you. You must decide whether or not you'll exchange a life of control born out of fear for a life of risk born out of faith..."*

If you could do anything you really wanted to do, what would you do? Start making a list of all the things, great and small, you deeply desire to do with your life. Don't ask yourself, "How?" *How* is not the right question for us; that is God's department. He is asking you "WHAT?" (Matthew 20:32). What is written on your heart? What makes you come alive? Just remember: God is the one who put that specific desire in your heart.

I moved to Los Angeles in 1987 with one thing on my mind ...making it as an actor. That single, burning desire consumed me at the time. Surprisingly, God used even my selfish hopes and desires to lead me to him. If I had not lived in Hollywood through some very hard times, I may never have found my church, my wife or my God.

Keep in mind that not every dream or desire we have reflects God's will for us. Romans 7-8 reminds us that the desires of our flesh wage war against the desires of God. We must match up our desires to God's Word. It can be tricky, but if something is not God's will, it will be made obvious to us as long as we remain connected to God and strive to maintain spiritual discernment and ask for advice (Proverbs 12:15).

Take the leap and give it 100% effort. If you do and it doesn't work out, then you have the contentment of knowing that it was truly not God's will. However, if you do not give it 100%, you will never know what God might have had for you right around the corner. The dream God placed in you and the talents to accomplish that dream are all right there inside you. You can live the dream!

FINDING YOUR SHAPE: Exploring Your Unique Purpose

Stuff to Talk Through With a Friend
* What activities and endeavors make your heart race?
* What would you do with your life if you could do anything you desired?
* What things do you seem to have talent or a special knack for?
* Who and what do you care about?

Things to Do If You Want to Grow
* Ask a good friend if they think you are doing God's will. Just ask.
* Write down a list of things that excite you…no matter what they are.
* Make a list of things that you are good at/things that come easy to you.

References for Further Bible Study
Jeremiah 29:11 • I Thessalonians 5:18 • Matthew 25:14-30 • I Corinthians 12:1-11 • Ephesians 4:11-13 • Romans 8:27, 12:2-8

Additional Resources
www.thedreamgiver.com
S.H.A.P.E. Finding and Fulfilling Your Unique Purpose for Life by Erik Reese
The Dream Giver by Bruce Wilkinson
Living Your Strengths by Albert Winseman, Donald Clifton and Curt Liesveld
Cure for the Common Life by Max Lucado
Spirit Controlled Temperament by Tim LaHaye
Discover Your God-Given Gifts by Don and Katie Fortune

For additional resources or to join our online community, go to:
http://fieldguide.faith21.org

Section Three
One Another

The Bible is full of instructions for dealing with life in community. When Jesus left, he never intended that we try to go it alone, but rather that we would be a family on earth that was a picture of the family we will be in Heaven. The following ten chapters will help you in dealing with those other sinners you call brother and sister.

> *Now you are together the body of Christ, and each of you is a part of it.*
> I Corinthians 12:27 (J.B. Phillips)

31

The Kingdom

Where Jesus Is King

> *Listen, my dear brothers: Has not God chosen those who are poor in the eyes of the world to be rich in faith and to inherit the kingdom he promised those who love him?*
> James 2:5

What is the Kingdom of God? Is it here now, or is it yet to come? If yet to come, where is it going to be?

There are many debates about these questions today, just as there were in the time of Jesus. For example, the Scribes and Pharisees thought about the Kingdom of God as a physical kingdom that would come if the people of Israel would follow God's law. If they could get enough people to meticulously observe the laws of God, he would then intervene by sending a king who would rid them of the Roman occupation and lead Israel as a sovereign nation. God would rule the world through Israel. The problem, as they saw it, was that there were not enough law-abiding Jews.

The Zealots believed the Kingdom would come through the rallying of Jews who were bold and decisive enough to organize an armed resistance. They would take their country back from the Romans, and then God would rule the world through Israel.

A third group of people thought that the Kingdom of God would come with visible signs. These were the "signs of the times" people, of which there are plenty today as well. They observed comets and astronomical phenomena, and meticulously attempted to dissect biblical prophecy.

All of these groups assumed that the Kingdom had to have a particular location. The location was "here," and the "here," of course, was Israel.

Jesus, responding to this controversy, goes for the jugular. In Luke 17:20, he says: "The coming of the Kingdom of God is not something that can be observed, nor will people say, 'Here it is,' or 'There it is,' because the Kingdom of God is in your midst." The reason why it was "in their midst" was because Jesus was in their midst. The Kingdom is not observable with the natural eye; nor defined by a location. It is here, and now; his name is Jesus. The Kingdom of God is everything, everywhere, everyone, every time where and when Jesus is king. The boundaries of this Kingdom do not lie in any geographic place, but in the hearts of true believers.

When I was young and living in a distant land, the Kingdom came to me through people who were different from anyone I had ever met before. These strange people exuded joy, refused to repay evil with evil and loved for no good reason (or so I thought). They were genuinely interested in my life, my past, my struggles and my fears. They crossed the boundaries of normal, social behavior, where people politely stay on the surface but don't really care. The Kingdom was at my doorstep, knocking, loving and advancing into my heart.

I resisted at first, being very skeptical of all organized religion. I doubted, having grown up all over the world and having seen so much human madness. I hesitated, knowing that my lifestyle would have to change. I was ashamed, being acutely aware of my sin; the selfish, arrogant and wicked person I was. Then, I found out that these people used to be all of that too, but Jesus died on the cross for them and rose again, to give them not only forgiveness, but his very Spirit and eternal life as new creations.

I will never forget the moment I made my decision to follow Jesus. A friend helping me study the Bible saw it without me telling him. "It seems to me you have already made your decision," he said. Was it written all over my face? Apparently yes. "I can't believe I am becoming a Christian. This is silly!" I thought to myself. But instead of voicing that, I said, "Do I have a choice?" My friend shook his head. He was right. How could I not follow, love and serve this Jesus? I couldn't hide my excitement. I desperately wanted to be part of this Kingdom, this invisible world where Jesus reigns supreme.

As Christians, our purpose is to manifest the Kingdom of God to the world around us. Being Jesus to whomever we are with effectively brings the Kingdom to them "right here, right now." We need to be Jesus to someone who is lost or addicted, to a person who betrays and slanders. We have to be the Kingdom to our gay neighbor, the elderly lady down the block who needs someone to talk to and the African orphan across the world who might not make it without our help. We really *can* be the Kingdom to our boring co-worker, the obviously promiscuous person in the gym, the homeless guy who stinks, the intimidating boss and the Muslim guy who doesn't seem like he would be into Jesus. Bring the Kingdom to the doorstep of their heart, and watch Jesus knock, love and advance.

The amazing thing is that the Kingdom of God is, in many ways, small, inconspicuous and humble. Jesus compares it to a mustard seed. However, the Kingdom does not stay small;

it grows and spreads like wildfire. A small woman, known as Mother Teresa, who became famous for her humble service to the poor in Calcutta, used to say, "In this life we cannot do great things. We can only do small things with great love." Her message of love did spread like wildfire, impacting generations of Christians and non-Christians alike.

The Kingdom is always right here and right now, and unlike the Pharisees, the Zealots and the "sign of the times" people, we need to always be aware that its source is from "another place." In John 18:36-37, Jesus said,

> "My kingdom is not of this world. If it were, my servants would fight to prevent my arrest by the Jewish leaders. But now my kingdom is from another place." "You are a king, then!" said Pilate. Jesus answered, "You say that I am a king. In fact, the reason I was born and came into the world is to testify to the truth. Everyone on the side of truth listens to me."

God is the source of this Kingdom we carry in our hearts. May we, who are "on the side of truth," while we go about our business, knowing that the Kingdom is "in our midst," listen attentively through the noise of this world for the loving voice of our King.

THE KINGDOM:
Where Jesus Is King

Stuff to Talk Through With a Friend
* In what ways does knowing that the Kingdom of God is "in our midst" help you?
* Can you think of any preconceived ideas, stereotypes or fears that stand in the way of your "Kingdom living?"
* What "little things with great love" are out there for you to manifest the Kngdom of God through?

Things to Do If You Want to Grow
* Create an environment where you can experience Jesus "in your midst." Reassess your relationship with God and people, your prayer life and your Bible study on a regular basis to experience Jesus' presence fully.
* When there is a person, situation or environment where you don't naturally engage, pray to overcome your preconceived ideas and stereotypes that keep you from manifesting the Kingdom of God to the world.

References for Further Bible Study
Matthew 21:31-43 • Mark 1:14-15, 4:11-34, 9:1, 9:45-50, 10:13-31 • Luke 13:20 • John 3:5-8 • Acts 1:3

Additional Resources
The Reign of God by Jim McGuiggan
Seeing Is Believing by Gregory Boyd
Thy Kingdom Come by Douglas Jacoby
All the Way to Kingdom Come by Thomas Jones/Steve Brown/S. Williams

For additional resources or to join our online community, go to:
http://fieldguide.faith21.org

32

A Short Church History

How Did We Get Here?

> "And I tell you that you are Peter, and on this rock I will build my church, and the gates of Hades will not overcome it."
>
> Matthew 16:18

In the beginning of the Christian movement, an assembly or congregation of disciples, referred to as *ecclesia* in Greek, formed in Jerusalem. The church, as it is now known, slowly broke off and spread to the surrounding areas in smaller groups (Acts 1:8). The word *church* accurately describes this body created by God, which is made up of believers who chose Christ as the leader or head of their lives (Colossians 1:16).

For the first eight to ten years, the church mainly consisted of Jews (Acts 11:1-18) who gathered in homes, outside synagogues and in a variety of other places. Many customs were kept from the Jewish heritage (Acts 3:1), but as the mission of the church began to include the Gentiles, the church changed to include this new diversity.

By the 100s AD, the idea of a universal or *catholic* church started unifying the family of God.[1] The body of Christ was

---

[1] Due to the brevity of this overview, specific references will not be provided. However, many of the facts can be found in the source material, listed in the reference section.

guided by the separate New Testament books being passed around, and by men called *Patristic,* or church fathers, who often had been mentored by the Apostles themselves. The church was not a building, but the family of God who emphasized loving God, loving one another, discipleship based on Christ and his teachings and evangelism (Acts 2:42-47). This focus, unfortunately, would not last.

In 313 AD, Emperor Constantine began legal toleration of Christianity, followed by the 381 AD decision by Theodosius I to make Christianity the official religion of the Roman Empire. Although these decisions gave disciples a new stance and freedom, the down side was that many people who were now "Christians" were not living the life.

During the 300s AD, forty-day Lent, candles, kissing the Bishop's hand and other rituals appeared which began a thousand years of traditions replacing an intimate relationship with God (Matthew 15:1-9). Additionally, the priests, a title given to elders in the 200s, were now paid by the Roman government. Magistrates enforced church decrees and all citizens were to be *christened*. The mainstream Christian model was becoming a whole new animal. The original teachings were becoming distorted, the church as the body of Christ was being seen as a mere building and an organic sense of the church with everyone participating was being replaced with an emphasis on *clergy*.

More and more traditions were creeping into the church. Leaders such as Augustine formulated the ideas of predestination, once saved always saved, original sin and infant baptism. Many of these concepts had negative effects on discipleship in the church.

By 1054, the universal church split for various reasons, with the West, or *Catholic*, speaking Latin, and the East, or *Orthodox*, speaking Greek. The unity of the church was broken, never to be restored. In the 1200s, Pope Innocent, seeing the need for unity, went so far as to declare torture acceptable in ensuring uniformity of doctrine and practice going forward. Of course, the very idea contradicted Christ's desire for love to be the sign of his church (John 13:34-35) and led to the horrendous inquisitions happening over the next few hundred years.

Partly as a reaction to the atrocities of the Catholic Church, the *Reformation* took root in the 1400s. The creation of the printing press in 1483 was monumental in fanning *Protestantism* because the Bible was given to the common man. Three main reformation leaders were Calvin, Zwingli and Luther who, in 1517, attached 95 theses (ideas that he believed the Bible called the Church to follow) to the church in Wittenberg's door—a familiar practice of the time. Luther's points spread widely and sparked a movement that had been waiting to be ignited.

Despite great intentions, the reformation was not a unifying time in Christian history. Wars broke out between countries claiming their own form of Christianity to be the *real* one. Catholic armies fought Protestants; Protestants attacked Protestants. Smaller groups called denominations emerged as churches of their own, all the time failing Christ's prayer and desire for unity (John 17:23).

In the late 1600s, a new movement started in the British Isles, and later in America, called the *Restoration* movement. This movement emphasized the first-century teachings and attempted to get away from traditions. Our family of churches today came out of this movement.

There were several men coming out of Protestantism who were influential in this movement in America. Barton Stone and Alexander Campbell were both front-runners of huge movements which united in 1831, and by 1848, the movement had many autonomous churches with around 200,000 members connected by various publications. An editor of one publication, David Lipscomb, became known as the "Father of the Churches of Christ." Unfortunately, unity was not to be found in this movement either as several splits happened over the years. After the Civil War, the more liberal churches in the North became the Disciples of Christ, while the conservative churches in the South became the Churches of Christ.

In the late 1960s and early 1970s, seventy years after this latest split, a new movement was initiated within the campus ministry, led by Chuck Lucas at the Crossroads Church of Christ in Florida. Lucas brought many new ideas for evangelism and discipleship, including prayer partners for accountability, confessing sins and mentoring. For evangelism, Lucas created Soul Talks, in which groups of 10-15 students would go on campus for an evangelistic Bible discussion. Many of our current church leaders were trained at Crossroads.

In the eighties, there was a movement out of Boston led by Kip McKean. Kip was converted and trained in Lucas' ministry at Crossroads in the early seventies. This group united many of the Crossroads trained leaders under McKean's leadership. While these leaders and churches wanted to take on the teachings of becoming a disciple, planting churches, discipleship partners and centralization of church leadership, other church leaders were critical of what they saw happening. The churches affiliated with the Boston Movement split off from the mainline, and it was in 1992 that *Church Growth Today* editor Dr. John Vaughn named these churches the "International Churches of Christ."

Ten years later, the leadership structure set up by McKean had evolved into a sometimes abusive, hierarchy of power within the church. This structure, along with overzealousness for immediate spiritual growth, hurt many people in our churches. As much of this came to light, the centralized leadership of our church was disbanded and many changes were introduced in order to provide healing and a more biblical climate of growth. In recent years, we have seen a renewal of faith, growth, spiritual health, humility and cooperation between our churches. God's Spirit is reaching a whole new generation of disciples in the 21st century!

Over time, the original church design experienced many alterations which have either moved people towards Christ and built up his church, or have led people away and caused divisions. Yet, through all these circumstances, disciples continue to live for God as God continues to draw his people to him. We are not the only Christians out there, but we are a movement motivated by God's grace to live by the Spirit, God's Word and God's plan for the church. History tells us there will be challenges again, but we are continually trying to build on the rock in order to fight through the coming storms (Matthew 16:16-18).

A SHORT CHURCH HISTORY: How Did We Get Here?

Stuff to Talk Through With a Friend
* How does the church's past relate to our current situation? What patterns do you see emerging?
* What strengths and weaknesses can you learn from church leaders in the past? How can your leadership grow from considering their lives?
* How do you see the Holy Spirit guiding your church now?

Things to Do If You Want to Grow
* Read up on one past church leader this year. Take notes on what you learn.
* Invest in books on the history of Christianity. Take a workshop or class on the topic.
* Form a group with others to discuss historical patterns in Christianity and in the church.
* Discuss current events which conflict with the purposes of the church and compare them with how the church dealt with past event problems in the Bible.

References for Further Bible Study
John 17 • Acts 4:32-35, 11:26 • Romans 12:4-5 • I Corinthians 3:1-9, 12:12-31 • Ephesians 1:22-23, 2:19-22, 3:6, 4:3-6, 4:11-16, 5:23, 5:29 • Colossians 1:15-20 • Hebrews 10:23-25

Additional Resources
Into all Nations by C. Foster Stanback
Introduction to History of Christianity by Tim Dowley
New Testament Survey by Merrill C. Tenney
Will the Real Heretic Please Stand Up? by David W. Bercot
A Dictionary of Early Christian Beliefs by David W. Bercot
Apostolic Fathers by J. R. Harmer and J.B. Lightfoot
Early Church History by David Bercot/Douglas Jacoby

For additional resources or to join our online community, go to:
http://fieldguide.faith21.org

33

Worship
A Way of Life

> *Ascribe to the LORD the glory due his name;*
> *worship the LORD in the splendor of his holiness.*
> **Psalm 29:2**

Worship is a term often misunderstood. The dictionary defines it as "reverent honor and homage paid to God." It can be a noun, as in "we attended *worship* today," or "we give you our *worship*," or it can be a verb, as in "we *worshipped* God today" or "he really *worships* that car." Paul gives us a great working definition: "Therefore, I urge you, brothers and sisters, in view of God's mercy, to offer your bodies as a living sacrifice, holy and pleasing to God—this is true worship" (Romans 12:1 TNIV). Worship is when we pause to remember who God is and what he has done for us, and then we respond.

One of the great mistakes of our generation has been to relegate worship to the music during a church service. Worship should go beyond Sunday morning into every moment of our lives—our relationships, our jobs, even our recreational time. Worship is our *response* to God's love for us. When we respond with kindness to a coworker's mean spirit, that is worship.

When we choose to engage with our kids instead of vegging out in front of the TV, that is worship. When we spend our time helping someone else learn about God, that is worship!

There is, however, a special focus on the music aspect of worship. As you grow in your Christian life, you may find that daily offering yourself as a living sacrifice is not always easy. In a brilliant move, God "commanded" to us to sing to the Lord and praise his name, because he is worthy of praise (Psalm 96:2-4). That is very true; he is worthy of all of our attention. However, we often see a "command" as something we "have to" do. But here's the beauty of it—when we sing to God, when we take time to remember his mercy, when we express it through song, *our* hearts start to change. God created music to engage a special, secret part of us that can soften our hearts and motivate us like nothing else can. As always, we find that God's command is actually for our benefit! How great is our God!

We must remember that, while we may benefit from our musical worship, it is not necessarily intended for our enjoyment. Worship is not about us. God did not tell us to sing praises to him so we could enjoy the music. So many opportunities to connect with God and what his Spirit is trying to tell us are missed because we are focusing on whether or not we like the music style of a particular song. In many cases, we will naturally enjoy the music that is played on Sunday mornings, but sometimes we may not. That is never the point, and Satan loves to get us distracted by musical criticism—as if we were *maestros of melody*. You can be sure that there are many reasons for the style of music and the songs that are chosen; in most churches, they are prayed over and thoughtfully selected. Whether we might be able to select better songs is never the point; we must start by remembering that the worship is designed to please God, not us.

Before crossing the Jordan and going to battle, Joshua told the people, "Consecrate yourselves, for tomorrow the LORD will do amazing things among you" (Joshua 3:5). In the same way, God wants us to prepare ourselves to worship him. God always wants to move in our hearts, but he cannot do it if he doesn't have our attention. That is why we spend time to remember God's love for us, and how incredibly blessed we are to be in his family. Pray that your vantage point would be "in view of God's mercy" before every worship service. Your worship will not be the same.

Some practical ideas to help with worship on Sundays:

* The music is not a warm-up to the "real" part of the service. It is our time to show God our love and affection.
* Be ready! Get to church early, find a great seat and be able to press "pause" on the thoughts of where you are going to eat after service.
* Don't let the music be a two-minute warning to end your conversation with someone. Choose to be waiting in eager anticipation for what God is going to do during the worship time.

When you worship, make sure your mind is engaged. Pay attention to the words that you are singing. Jesus tells us to "Love the Lord your God with all your heart and with all your soul and with all your mind and with all your strength" (Mark 12:30). Part of loving God with your mind is actively thinking about the words you are singing and how they apply to your life. If you find yourself just singing words without thinking about them, you are slipping into religious rituals that have no meaning. No matter what the style of music, or if you like the song, virtually every song will have some truth, some encouraging thought, some wonderful expression of praise that you can sing with all of your mind!

Not all of the benefit of musical worship enters through the mind. I often feel my heart moved by God as I am singing in worship. God will bring a situation to mind that he wants me to surrender to him, or give me a sense of excitement about a particular person or situation. Many times, it has also been a great time of confession for me. Listen for God to speak to you and allow your heart to be moved as you listen for God's voice.

Few things can affect us as deeply as music. When you combine the power of music with the power of showing reverent honor and homage to God, you have an amazing result. Musical worship can be one of the most spiritually fulfilling activities of your life. We can then let that inspiration move us toward true worship of God in *every* area of our lives, as a response to all that God has done for us.

WORSHIP: A Way of Life

Stuff to Talk Through With a Friend
* Do I come to worship services ready to give to God, or am I expecting to be given to?
* Am I able to engage my mind, even on songs that may not be my favorites?
* How can I prepare differently for a service so that I can connect with God on a deeper level?

Things to Do If You Want to Grow
* Figure out what kind of worship music is your favorite, or which artists you really like, then fill up your iPod with those songs. Listen to them on the way to work, at home while making dinner, anytime you can to keep your heart in a constant state of worship, and be able to enjoy your particular favorites, even if you don't get them at church.
* If you are musically inclined, compose your own Psalm music. Take one of your favorites from the Bible, and put music to it.
* Pray during the service, between the songs, for God to move in the hearts of the congregation.
* Allow your worship to be a witness. Smile when you sing, close your eyes, sing directly to God. Your children and the friends you bring with you to church will be impacted by your example. Don't put on a show, but give your whole heart to God.

References for Further Bible Study
Psalm 92:1-4, 95:1-7, 96, 98, 100, 103 • John 4:23-24 • I Corinthians 14:22-25 • Revelation 4:8-11

Additional Resources
The Air I Breathe by Louie Giglio
Indescribable and *How Great is Our God* DVDs by Louie Giglio
The Unquenchable Worshipper by Matt Redman

For additional resources or to join our online community, go to:
http://fieldguide.faith21.org

34

Fellowship
Do I Really Need to Be Connected?

> *The eye cannot say to the hand, "I don't need you!"*
> *And the head cannot say to the feet, "I don't need you!"*
> I Corinthians 12:21

The privilege of fellowship with God is a reward beyond comprehension, but he does not stop there. He gives us an eternal family as well. Fellowship is experiencing life together as one body. We truly are blessed as believers because God provides for us in every way. There is no shortage of ways we get to spend time with each other: church services, baptisms, birthday parties, conferences, family celebrations and memorials. The list goes on. Fellowship is fun and a necessary part of enjoying the life God intended us to live (II John 4:11-12).

We need each other. A lone believer is not part of God's plan. He tells us that our faith is shown in how we love one another (John 13:34). One of the first times I visited church, I was invited to lunch afterwards at the home of a believer I didn't even know. She was very hospitable and cooked chili for about 20 of her friends—plus me. This act of service left a huge impression on me. She really loved her friends and expressed such joy to be able to give to them using her talents in the kitchen. I remember that experience more than I remember the sermon that day. It inspired me to continue attending church and observing the believers. Everyone would greet each other with big hugs. They all smiled and were sincerely glad to see each other!

"The way God designed our bodies is a model for understanding our lives together as a church: every part dependent on every other part, the parts we mention and the parts we don't, the parts we see and the parts we don't. When living together in a healthy way, all the body parts function according to their purpose. For example, if one part hurts, every other part is involved in the hurt. If one part flourishes, every other part enters into the exuberance" (I Corinthians 12:12-27—The Message).

The key to fellowship is being together as one body. We need to be connected because we were all uniquely created with a purpose that will support the other parts to work correctly. If we are not aware of how we are connected and needed, everyone suffers and the body has to improvise. When we have to pick something up with our toes, it is a little harder than just using our hands. We need to stay connected because none of the parts of the body can replace nor do the job of another body part.

Healthy fellowship is one that has Christ's blood running through it. We can hang out together, but without faith in God, it is wasted time. When we are united in faith, we are a powerful force to be reckoned with (Hebrews 11:30). Every cell in the body gets its nutrients from blood. When getting a check-up from a doctor, blood is the most commonly tested part of the body, for it is truly the river of life. In the same way, we share the lifeline with each other by letting Jesus' healing blood run through us in order to reach all the body parts (John 15:5; Hebrews 13:20-21). How can we do this? By meeting together regularly and helping one another to obey God's Word with all our hearts.

True, genuine relationships are the result of fellowship. A great example of intimate fellowship in my life is no matter whom I live with, those Christians end up being my closest friends. They are the ones that see me at my best and at my worst, both spiritually and physically. They are the ones who can encourage me the most and meet my needs the best. On the other hand, they are the people that can hurt me the deepest because my heart is acutely vulnerable to their words and actions. Without friends who are willing to "speak the truth in love" (Ephesians 4:15) and study the Bible with me (Hebrews 4:12), my life would be completely different right now. Jesus' provision of family and my choice to immerse myself in the fellowship have given me purpose. I no longer live for myself, lost in the dark.

Jesus sacrificed his life so that we could be redeemed and restored to the family of God. You belong. You were "wonderfully made" (Psalm 139:14), and God desires you (Romans 3:23-26)! He has given us the responsibility to be ambassadors of reconciliation by spreading the gospel (II Corinthians 5:19-20; Matthew 28:16). We can only accomplish this task if we work together as one body.

For all of these reasons, each of us needs to be involved in a small group within the church. We must be connected to the other parts we so desperately need. We are not alone because he created us to be a family both physically and spiritually. Being a fellowship means actively living out all the "one another" commands in the Bible. Talk about this list with a friend. Are you practicing them?

Do not deceive one another - Leviticus 19:11
Show mercy and compassion to one another - Zechariah 7:9
Be devoted to one another - Romans 12:10
Live in harmony with one another - Romans 12:16, 1 Peter 3:8
Accept one another - Romans 15:7
Instruct one another - Romans 15:14
Agree with one another - I Corinthians 1:10
Greet one another with a holy kiss - II Corinthians 13:12
Serve one another in love - Galatians 5:13
Bearing with one another in love - Ephesians 4:2
Be kind and compassionate to one another - Ephesians 4:32
Speak to one another with psalms, hymns and spiritual songs - Ephesians 5:19
Submit to one another out of reverence for Christ - Ephesians 5:21
Admonish one another - Colossians 3:16
Encourage one another - 1 Thessalonians 5:11, Hebrews 3:13, Hebrews 10:25
Spur one another on toward love and good deeds - Hebrews 10:24
Do not slander one another - James 4:11
Offer hospitality to one another without grumbling - 1 Peter 4:9
Love one another deeply - 1 Peter 1:22
Clothe yourselves with humility toward one another - 1 Peter 5:5

FELLOWSHIP:
Do I Really Need to Be Connected?

Things to Do If You Want to Grow
* Look up every "one another" scripture in the Bible and write down either an example of how you are currently obeying that scripture or what you need to do in order to obey that scripture for each one.
* Ask several spiritual friends what your strengths and weaknesses are and just listen to their answers humbly without giving excuses or defending yourself.
* Take someone in your church to lunch whom you have never hung out with before and spend some quality time with them listening to their needs and dreams.

References for Further Bible Study
Hebrews 10:25 • Romans 12: 3-8 • Colossians 3:15-16 • James 2:14-18 • Galatians 6:10 • Ephesians 4 • Matthew 25:34-40 • I John 3:16-18

Additional Resources
The Purpose Driven Life by Rick Warren
The Love Languages of God by Gary Chapman
The Lord of the Rings Trilogy by J. R. R. Tolkien
Like a Tree Planted by Streams of Water by G. Steve Kinnard

For additional resources or to join our online community, go to:
http://fieldguide.faith21.org

35

Creating Family
Life in a Small Group

> *For this reason, I kneel before the Father, from whom his whole family in heaven and on earth derives its name.*
> **Ephesians 3:15**

The word most often associated with a Christian small group is "family." Christians are all "brothers" and "sisters" in "Father" God's family (II Corinthians 6:18). The frame of reference we use to define family is our own. How we relate to our spiritual siblings, including big brother Jesus, is greatly influenced by how we relate to our physical family. Take a moment to evaluate your own family. No matter how your family raised you, God has his own ideas of what a family, especially his spiritual family, is to be like in the way we treat each other.

God sets the lonely in families (Psalm 68:6). Why a family and not a business, or a therapy group? Why should a Christian small group be a family? Just as marriage is an example of our relationship with God and church is our example of heaven, a small group can be viewed as a small example of the family of God. Is it perfect? Of course not. We live in a broken world, and

God knows that. Perfection is not the goal. The goal of a small group is to experience the splendor of what a family means to God.

What does God want us to experience in his family? Study Jesus' prayer in John 17, the last public prayer before his crucifixion, and you will see what type of family God wants. First and foremost, he wants us to experience intimacy with him and each other through unity. Unity is the glue that keeps a family together, through commitment, purpose, and protection. A small group must have these three elements of unity if it is to truly reflect God's larger family.

Acting Like Family

Regardless of why you first joined a small group, God now has you in a training arena. It is in *this* school where you learn how to apply the concepts of family and love in real relationships. Here, commitment to the group becomes crucial. Don't for a second think that any person in your group is there by accident, or by a leader's design, because God himself indicated that "as iron sharpens iron, so one man sharpens another" (Proverbs 27:17). You are in the group to teach and learn from each of the other individuals in the group, and to collectively rescue the souls of the lost around you. Every member is important. Commitment teaches us that the group and the members in it are more valuable than any temporary hurts we may cause each other in the normal course of interpersonal relationships. We stick together because we are God's children. This fact should bond us in the conviction that each person is invaluable and should be treated that way, regardless of any conflicts.

God also wants his family to experience unity through purpose. Having a common purpose bonds people together, and one of the most powerful unifying goals in Christianity is the Great Commission (Matthew 28:19-20) by which we individually and collectively work to help others come to know God. He gives us this common goal to unite us for a common cause.

Hospitality is a powerful avenue for a small group to express its commitment and purpose to the world. Hospitality reveals the power of God working in the lives of the members in a way that people in the world long to see. Each member of a family should want to share the special privilege of family with those who may not have it.

Another purpose of unity is protection. "Two are better than one," Ecclesiastes 4 tells us, and it has proven true time after time. Satan is our enemy. He is also the destroyer of all that God creates, including his family. One way to thwart him is to watch out for each other and protect each other. Hebrews 3:13 commands us to encourage one another as a defense against the deceitfulness of sin. Family life helps us to encourage one another daily to live and be like Jesus (Romans 1:12). If we are committed to each other and share the goal of showing God to the world, we will want to go out of our way to protect each other from Satan's schemes.

Commitment and encouragement help a family cope in difficult times. Knowing that each member is really there for the other members can offer hope against the lie that we are alone. The encouragement each member gives, and the determination to give it even when there are problems in our own lives, is the glue that shows us that God is the one who really keeps us alive spiritually.

Dealing Like Family

Every family has problems; spiritual ones are not

exceptions to the rule. Conflicts are common, but God has a plan for dealing with them that does not tear the group apart or damage the members. As selfish humans, we usually take one of two approaches when trouble comes: fight or flight. Some people turn on others and attack back when they feel attacked. Others run away and refuse to deal with the issues. Neither way benefits God or the family; rather, it is profitable only for Satan, who wants to destroy the family in any way he can. When the inevitable conflict arises, Satan prods us to take a wrong path.

Philippians 2:3-4 is the guiding light in dealing with family conflicts. Simply put, this passage teaches us to treat one another with humility, and other people as better than ourselves. That is a tough stand to take, but you can live this way if you have a firm resolve for family unity. Commitment reminds you that you and the other person are equal in value in God's eyes. Protection reminds you of who the enemy is when you are being manipulated into fighting with another member. Purpose reminds you that there are needs in the world more desperate than yours.

A family, or a small group, is not a utopian micro-society. It is as imperfect as we are individually. Only with God's strength and his focus on unity will we be the type of family that moves us and those in the world toward God. With God and his family, we can do immeasurably more (Ephesians 3:20).

CREATING FAMILY:
Life in a Small Group

Stuff to Talk Through With a Friend
* What is your role in your small group? How can you play a more significant part in the lives of the others?
* What has your physical family taught you about the concept of "family"? How does it compare with what the Bible teaches?
* Think of a person in your group you have a conflict with. What would committing to them, sharing a purpose with them and protecting them look like in a practical way?

Things to Do If You Want to Grow
* Pray specific prayers for each person in your group every day for a week. If you don't have specifics to pray for, ask them.
* Commit to contacting each person in your group, as appropriate, before the end of each week.
* Find a topic for which the whole group can do a personal Bible study. Meet together in twos or threes to study together. Do it for a month.
* Meet together for prayer times and faith-sharing times on a consistent basis.

References for Further Bible Study
John 13:34-35 • Romans 12:10, 13:8 • I Peter 1:22, 3:8

Additional Resources
Simple Church: Returning to God's Process for Making Disciples by Thom S. Rainer, Eric Geiger

Creating Community: Five Keys to Building a Small Group Culture by Andy Stanley, Bill Willits

A Model for Making Disciples: John Wesley's Class Meeting by D. Michael Henderson

For additional resources or to join our online community, go to:
http://fieldguide.faith21.org

36

Conflict Resolution
Doing It God's Way

> *Make every effort to keep the unity of the Spirit through the bond of peace.*
> **Ephesians 4:3**

Resolving conflict is one of the most important things we can learn as young Christians. If this ability is not a part of our character, we will go through life causing havoc in our relationships and creating unnecessary emotional turmoil. When this capacity *is* in our character, we can cultivate deep friendships and manage tension in a productive way (James 3:18).

God has created people with a variety of personalities and different purposes, even in the church (I Corinthians 12:12-31). When dealt with in a mature fashion of respect and acceptance, these differences help us to grow (Romans 14:1-15:7). In fact, God creates these opportunities under his guidance (I Corinthians 10:10), and puts us in relationships in order to mature us (Proverbs 27:17).

The way I have handled certain conflicts as a Christian has been...well, let me just say...not very mature. One time, a friend and I were leading a ministry together, and we were trying to make a decision on how to organize the launch night. I wanted to have a concrete plan before enlisting other people to serve, and he wanted to go ahead and call people first to let them know they were involved. Because of our inability to resolve conflict, we began to hurt each other's feelings. I kept pushing to achieve my agenda, refusing to collaborate or even admit my feelings. This left my counterpart feeling manipulated, not valued and not listened to. The discussion intensified, and I became upset and just wanted to escape the whole situation. All of this happened because I did not know how to work in a positive way through the tension I was feeling.

Other times, my thoughts and emotions raced around inside me, keeping me from focusing on the tasks at hand. I had several imaginary conversations going on in my head at the same time. These thoughts and feelings would then be unleashed upon someone whenever the "last straw" broke. All of these situations have been the result of my inability to resolve conflict.

So how can we resolve conflict in a righteous way?

We should start by considering the other person's interests first, instead of our own (Philippians 2:4). This will provide an opportunity to work as a team. Entire conflicts can be avoided in this way, and if not, at least our friends' concerns and perspective will have been communicated. This will help them feel validated and open to seeing our point of view. Also, we might realize the value of working together instead of by ourselves.

When conversations intensify, as they often do, we must take the time to admit what we are feeling. If we are not sure of what we are feeling, it is a good idea to take a small break from the situation. Then, we can pray and quickly connect with ourselves to help make things clear (James 4:2).

Next, do not follow my example and continue to push for what you want. Share with the other person how you are hurt (Matthew 18:15, 5:23-24), and do it with a spirit of honesty and love (Ephesians 4:15). A great way to do this (Ephesians 4:25) is to use the word "I" instead of "you." Using statements such as "*I* was really hurt, *I* felt I wasn't being listened to" is a less offensive way to communicate than "*you* hurt my feelings when *you* did not listen to me."

If you cannot work through the conflict immediately, you should set up a meeting in a comfortable and neutral place. Allow for plenty of time to talk and listen to each other, and remember that the problem is what you want to focus on, not the person. When you talk through the problem, be prepared to admit your own fault in the situation (Matthew 7:3-5). Just a hint—you probably will not know what your fault is until the other person points it out. Also, have the humility to realize you may not have communicated lovingly. One way to be humble is to connect with how the other person is feeling. Often, we get caught up with our thoughts instead of the other person's feelings. If we knew how the other person was feeling, things might have gone very differently.

Depending on the disagreement, conflict can sometimes be worked out by merely sympathizing and understanding why the other person is hurt. If a person is still nursing a wound, they are going to have a difficult time dealing with any other thoughts (Psalm 73:21-22).

After someone shares what they are feeling, repeat back to them what you heard, focusing on the hurt feelings. Then ask if there is any part that you missed. For example, you could sincerely say, "It sounds like you were hurt by the way I snapped at you. Is there anything else I did that hurt you?" If you are not sincerely and humbly trying to resolve the problem, the other person will continue to feel hurt as you talk.

Finally, take the time to honestly apologize for however you have hurt the other person. Taking responsibility lets the other person know you are serious. An apology will restore your friendship and help solve the problem. After you have exchanged apologies, continue to work out the conflict until you both feel good about the situation.

In a world characterized by turmoil and dysfunction, you can prosper in unity by resolving conflict God's way. He designed relationships to build one another up, not to tear each other down (Ephesians 4:16). Choose to be a part of his plan. When feelings or thoughts are expressed, consider the interests of others first. Strive to be a great friend by being honest, sharing your feelings in a loving way and being humble enough to admit when you are wrong. God loves to watch you resolve conflict righteously because he knows it can breed intimacy (John 21:15-19).

CONFLICT RESOLUTION: Doing It God's Way

Stuff to Talk Through With a Friend
* Is there someone you do not feel resolved with right now? What do you feel unresolved about?
* Are you feeling hurt by anyone right now? How long have you felt this way?
* Are there any recurring situations that breed conflict or where you feel like you are unsure how to handle the rising tension?

Things to Do If You Want to Grow
* Journal your feelings daily. This will help you be more in touch.
* Find an accountability partner and study out resolving conflict. Share your findings with them.
* Also meet with him or her consistently to get input on how you can handle conflict more effectively.

References for Further Bible Study
Matthew 5:9, 6:14, 22:39 • Luke 11:1-4, 17:4 • I Corinthians 13 • Ephesians 4:2-3, 4:29 • Colossians 3:1-17

Additional Resources
Connecting by Larry Crabb
Changes that Heal by Dr. Henry Cloud
Boundaries by Dr. Henry Cloud and Dr. John Townsend
Five Languages of Apologies by Dr. Gary Chapman
Making Peace by Jim Van Yperen
Firestorm by Ron Susek
The DNA of Relationships by Gary Smalley

For additional resources or to join our online community, go to:
http://fieldguide.faith21.org

37

Christian Dating
It Isn't Just About Finding a Spouse

> *Do nothing out of selfish ambition or vain conceit, but in humility consider others better than yourselves. Each of you should look not only to your own interests, but also to the interests of others.*
> **Philippians 2:3-4**

Reading that dating isn't about finding a spouse may come as a shock to you. We are living in a world that has indoctrinated us into believing that the only way to find marital happiness is to date and date and date, and if you don't date, you'll never get married. It's also the reason that almost all married couples stop dating once the rings are on the fingers. This should not be the case.

The point of dating is just like the point to every other relationship-oriented activity in life: to move both of your hearts closer to God. That is the primary and most important reason to date. To most of us, this seems unrealistic. If that's all there is to dating, what's so special about it, then?

Motives are the key. Why do you date in the first place? Is it usually so that you can get something out of it? That reveals your motives. Now, put your own motives on the shelf for a minute and consider—what does God want for you from a date? Since you are dating his son or daughter, it's safe to think he wants you to treat them with the highest priority, not yourself. Philippians 2:3 tells us to consider others better than ourselves. God wants his children to feel like they are special. Guess what? That's the job God is giving you when he lets you date his child!

God wants the person you date to be treated as his son, or daughter, and that means even after you are married. No Christian married couple should ever stop dating. The same motives and benefits in dating apply after marriage. It's not about getting something you want, like a wedding. It's about you giving something to the person God put in your life, whether it is for one night, or every night for the rest of your lives.

An important question in dating is: whom should you date? Again, it all comes back to your motives. When you are single, you are free to date anyone you want. There are biblical principles to be aware of, however, namely the principle of the yoke. We are created with a social nature. Emotional attachments, or yokes, are naturally created from chemical processes in our brain. We are literally wired for relationships. Therefore, the more interaction we have with a particular person, the stronger the attachment becomes. Dating is a socially acceptable way to form these attachments between men and women. This natural attachment is augmented by our society's one-track goal of mate seeking. Unless there is a safety in place, an emotional attachment can easily be forged between people who are spiritually damaging to each other.

The principle of the yoke in II Corinthians 6:14 states the obvious that anyone who does not share your goals in life, especially spiritual goals, is an unequal yoke. If you follow Christ and they follow themselves, eventually either the relationship destroys itself, or the more dominant personality will win over. Unfortunately, most often it is the Christian who gives in. Once a Christian willfully goes against God's Word, he or she has started down a road that can only lead to disaster. On the other hand, dating someone who is proven by their lifestyle and choices, not just their intentions or flowery language, to be a Christian, means that no matter what God plans in the future for the relationship, both will be drawn closer to him.

Do we even know how to go on a date? Many of us consider ourselves to be pros at dating, but we must realize that our experiences in the past may not have prepared us to date in a righteous way.

First of all, if you are single, a double date is the most advisable way to date. This may seem old fashioned, but remember, Satan is your enemy and will turn dating into an all out war if you refuse to heed the warnings. Everything *is* permissible, as it says in I Corinthians 10:23. If you want to go on a date with just the two of you, then you can. You are an adult, and as a Christian, you have the Holy Spirit in you. However, not everything is beneficial (I Corinthians 10:24). Satan knows how your brain works better than you do, and he knows all of your weaknesses. Building a relationship, even a spiritual one, on an emotional attachment is a dangerous game. Again, check your motives. Who is it that really wants the attachment to get stronger—you or God? If you believe it is God, then you can follow even the most out-of-touch rules that exist, and the relationship will still blossom. However, if you are the one pushing for the attachment, then having another set of eyes, someone to watch your back, will alert you and keep both you and your date safe.

Much can be made of religious rules and dating. Since

there is no biblical precedent, then dating has to be governed by other principles, such as the *one another* principle, the *God-first* principle, and the *love* principle. The only real rules in dating are: 1) don't make it about you; and 2) don't focus on it as your path to marriage.

I was trapped in a cycle of selfish dating for over 12 years as a Christian. These principles were familiar to me, but I thought they were meant for someone else. I wanted to get married. The right girl was never there for me, and I blamed God. Then, I read Genesis 24 and compared Isaac's plan for marriage against my own. He did *nothing* to get his bride (read it for yourself) and I was doing everything I could think of—and failing. I had to own up to my selfish motives in dating. Once I did, God blessed me with my beautiful wife. Let go of your desire to be married and simply date other Christians for *their* sake. Then stand back and watch God do great things for you and them.

CHRISTIAN DATING:
It Isn't Just About Finding A Spouse

Stuff to Talk Through With a Friend
* What is your dating life like currently? What are your reasons for dating, or not dating?
* Which extreme do you gravitate to—desperate to get married or resisting all such relationships? How does your past experience affect your current state?
* What would a date look like with absolutely no conditions except giving to the other person? How could you make that happen?
* How can you have a relationship with a Christian of the opposite gender and not get tangled in relationship issues?

Things to Do If You Want to Grow
* Plan a date with a Christian whom you have absolutely no romantic interest in. Serve them the way Jesus would if he were on the date.

References for Further Bible Study
Romans 12:10, 15:1-2 • I Corinthians 10:24 • Ephesians 5:21

Additional Resources
I Kissed Dating Goodbye by Joshua Harris
Mars and Venus on a Date by John Gray
Friiends and Lovers by Sam and Geri Laing

For additional resources or to join our online community, go to:
http://fieldguide.faith21.org

38

Finding That Special One
What to Do While Waiting

> *Love must be sincere.*
> Romans 12:9

In Genesis, we read how God gave Adam work to do, a beautiful place to live, and a life of security and simple pleasures (Genesis 1 and 2). And yet Adam was lonely and needed his "special someone." Yet Adam never had to go searching for a perfect match. God met his need and introduced Adam to his future wife, Eve. In some ways, Adam had it made. It was pretty clear that God had chosen Eve as his mate; her eye wasn't also on some other fellow. Anytime Eve was all dolled up, he knew it was especially for him. Today, we have the benefit of more dating options, but much less certainty. Nervous questions flood our brains. "Is it God's plan that I marry?" "How will I know the right one?" "Will that person know I'm the right one?" And the horror of horrors, "What if I never get married?" Adam's story teaches us that the desire for a spouse is natural and good, but sometimes we go about fulfilling this need in the wrong way.

The search for that "special someone" should begin and end with surrender. This means seeking and willingly submitting to God's will. Romantic surrender involves accepting and being content with the possibility of lifetime singleness. Jesus, Jeremiah, Elijah, Miriam and Lydia were all single. It is not God's plan for everyone to marry (Jeremiah 16:2). Paul didn't even want a wife, (I Corinthians 7:7) and in Romans 16 commends many lesser-known single Christians. Marriage is a gift from God, but unlike Heaven, it is not promised to anyone who follows Jesus. Without surrender in this area, we essentially hold God hostage to our expectations, or take over his job as provider by trying to "find" our own mate. For if God is not enough, neither will be any man or woman.

The prime pitfall of Christians in building relationships with the opposite sex is worldly games, commonly reflected in three basic patterns. In the first scenario, we selectively offer our hearts only to those whom we "like." If no relationship comes to pass with the objects of our affection, the friendships dissolve. The second prototype finds us offering "friendship only" to someone until sensing an interest from that someone, who may not be our type. We then withdraw, leaving a good-intentioned Christian hurt and bewildered. We justify this action with the claim of "protecting" the other's heart. In reality, withdrawing is simply making sure that someone knows we're not romantically interested in a very cowardly way. Finally, there's the relationship destroyer: "Like me back or I will completely avoid eye contact with you for the rest of my life." Yikes! All of the above are both immature and unspiritual, springing from fear, selfishness and a lack of faith. On and on, these cycles repeat, leaving nearly non-existent friendships between unattached singles.

The dating-game dysfunction, even within our churches,

can create unnecessary scars. Few of us qualified as role models of any kind prior to becoming Christians, yet we have allowed our fractured dating habits to accompany us into the church. In Matthew 28:20, Jesus directs us to teach one another everything. No matter our physical age or experience when becoming Christians, we need the humility to learn godly dating. The good news is that the solution does not require extraordinary abilities, only the willingness to surrender. By applying a bit of sound advice, your relationships will become a source of joy and fulfillment, and staying surrendered to God will be infinitely easier. Want to know what it is?

Give your heart to everyone, all the time, every day, until you die (II Corinthians 6:11-13). Obviously, you must use discernment and maintain healthy boundaries. However, if there are no huge red flags, give your heart.

Sound risky? It is! To do so is to imitate Jesus, who, regardless of the response, continually offered his heart to all. A Christian should not open his heart to some and withhold it from others. Philippians 2:4 should be applied to all areas of the Christian life, including dating; "Each of you should look not only to your own interests, but also to the interests of others." Though it is quite natural to have a list of preferences in a potential mate, the danger lies in presuming that God's plan aligns with our tastes. God know us better than we know ourselves (Psalm 139:1), and sometimes God's plan is not what we expect. It is doubtful that the adulterous Gomer made Hosea's prospective-wife list, but God unexpectedly called for him to marry her (Hosea 1:2-3)! As a single, I learned to be open to any sister as my future wife or good friend. I wanted to build the best female friendships possible. The fact is, I was rejected a LOT; I may hold the world record! The vast majority of women opted to become my good friend. But these rejections took the form of great brother-sister friendships, and this kind of rejection leaves no scars. I can tell you with certainty that I hit the jackpot by letting God pick my wonderful wife!

One note of caution: Christians should only date and marry other Christians (II Corinthians 6:14-17). The futility of unequally yoked couples is displayed in various marriages in the Bible: Abigail (I Samuel 25:14-15) and Samson (Judges 16:1-20) are prime examples. Marriages between a Christian and a non-Christian will absolutely not work. It might seem harmless fun to date someone in the world who is fun and has a genuine interest in you, but the inherent dangers are so hazardous that it should never be attempted.

Remember, we are building up the church (I Corinthians 12:12), and each of us has a part to play. We must protect one another's hearts through consistent giving, as Jesus did. By putting God first (Psalm 37:4), giving unconditionally (James 2:1), praying (I Thessalonians 5:17) and seeking wise counsel (Proverbs 19:20), we're sure to discover God's perfect will for our spouse. That is the victory of surrender!

FINDING THAT SPECIAL ONE:
What to Do While Waiting

Stuff to Talk Through With a Friend
* Are you willing to go on dates with those whom you are not physically attracted to?
* Would you go on a date with someone whom you knew was not physically attracted to you?
* Why are women instructed to be modest?
* Why are men instructed to be providers and protectors?
* Are you willing to joyfully remain faithful to God if you never get married?

Things to Do If You Want to Grow
* Pray to be surrendered to God's will.
* Make a decision to give your heart to everyone without considering what you stand to gain or to lose.
* Encourage others by setting them up with other Christian friends. Even if there is no compatibility, people enjoy being thought about.
* Research and study the lives of lifelong biblical singles and couples.

References for Further Bible Study
Judges 14:3 • Matthew 19:1-12 • Romans 12:9 • Romans 16 (entire chapter) • I Corinthians 7 (entire chapter) • James 4:1-3

Additional Resources
Wild at Heart: Discovering the Secrets of a Man's Soul by John Eldredge
Captivating: Unveiling the Mystery of a Woman's Soul by John and Staci Eldredge
I Kissed Dating Goodbye: A New Attitude Toward Dating by Josh Harris

For additional resources or to join our online community, go to:
http://fieldguide.faith21.org

39

Marriage
The Roles God Designed Us to Play

> *What is clearest to me is the way Christ treats the church. And this provides a good picture of how each husband is to treat his wife, loving himself in loving her, and how each wife is to honor her husband.*
> **Ephesians 5:29-33 (The Message)**

One of the most exciting things in becoming a Christian is the hope Jesus provides for having a great marriage that will last for a lifetime! Sadly, most of us grew up in broken homes where our parent's marriage either dissolved into divorce, or just grew cold and unappealing over time. It is rare indeed to have the privilege of being raised with a healthy, positive example of a godly marriage, where mom and dad love God and each other. Even rarer are homes where biblical roles are lived out in such a way as to inspire our own outlook on marriage. Thankfully, when we make Jesus the Lord of our lives, he begins a renewal of our minds and hearts, giving us hope where there has been little before.

From the beginning of time, God's intent was to bless us through marriage. Eve was a gift for Adam in every way: a helper, friend, confidant, lover and companion to enjoy life with. Proverbs 18:22 says, "He who finds a wife finds what is good and receives favor from the LORD." What a tragedy that such a blessing could become so degraded by our modern society. Marriage is mocked by the media, cheapened by "one night stands" and weakened by our society's ever growing self-centered mentality. Yet even through it all, we long for this relationship that has been hardwired into our DNA since creation.

We will never make marriage work without putting God first. He must be the Lord of every area of our lives, including marriage. His role as the head is essential: "Now I want you to realize that the head of every man is Christ, and the head of the woman is man, and the head of Christ is God" (I Corinthians 11:3). Without God as the head of a marriage, it will surely fail. But with God leading, we have nothing to fear as we actively submit our marriage to God. Practical ways you can put God first in your marriage are praying together daily and always turning to the scriptures during disagreements. Also, make a vow to never mention divorce, no matter how bad the situation gets. "'I hate divorce', says the LORD God of Israel…So guard yourself in your spirit, and do not break faith" (Malachi 2:15). We must actively seek God's will for our marriage through prayer and the scriptures, and close the back door once and for all.

Marriage was God's invention, and as with everything he created, it works when we follow his instructions. Embracing the roles that God has set up for marriage will help you to strengthen the foundation of your marriage in these early days of your Christian walk. The husband has a role in marriage that is well defined. In Ephesians 5:25-33, God calls the husband to act as the head, or leader, of his wife just as Christ is the head of the Church; to love his wife as Jesus loved us. There is truly no greater calling in all of scripture.

Our modern society may scoff at the idea of a man leading his wife, but looking more closely, we can see the beauty of God's plan. A husband, submitted to the Lordship of Christ, accepts the responsibility of leadership for his family and willingly lays down his life for his wife, putting her needs before his own. Obviously, God's idea of leadership is quite different from that of our society. A man willing to step up and lead his wife toward God is a noble man indeed.

In the same passage written to husbands, God addresses the role of wives in two short sentences: "Wives, submit to your husbands as to the Lord...and the wife must respect her husband."

God calls wives to follow their husbands and treat them with respect. The very idea of "submission" is not popular these days, and a woman willingly submitting to any man is almost scandalous. But here again, God's view of submission is quite different than that of our society. First of all, God does not view "following" as less than "leading"; quite the opposite, Jesus tells us that Heaven has a very different importance scale than what we use (Matthew 20:26, 23:11). More importantly, Jesus' example shows us that we all, men and women alike, must learn the art of submission (Hebrews 5:7). The submissive role God has given a wife allows her day-in and day-out practice to become like Jesus.

In effect, God created Christian marriage as an absolutely foolproof method of helping us to grow. The role he gave the husband goes against his natural tendency to selfishly sit back and be passive; man is commanded to lead and to love sacrificially, like Jesus. The role he gave the wife also goes against her nature. A woman naturally wants to control her environment and lead the way; God commands her to submit to her husband's leadership and respect him, even when he doesn't deserve respect. Why would God purposely join two people who are so different and then give them roles that go against their natural inclinations? As John and Stasi Eldredge write in the book *Love and War*:

"Why would God do such a thing? Because marriage is a divine conspiracy. It is a conspiracy arranged and with divine intent. God lures us into marriage…and then he uses it to transform us."

When God created marriage, he said "the two shall become one." Like beautiful ballroom dancers gliding across the dance floor seamlessly, when we embrace the roles given to us, our marriage can be a flawless example of God's perfect plan. However, when we fight against God's plan, we start to step on each other's feet. Dancing well takes practice, so get out and dance to the rhythm of God's plan.

MARRIAGE:
The Roles God Designed Us to Play

Stuff to Talk Through With a Friend
* How do you honestly view the roles that God has assigned in marriage?
* Ask your friend how their view of marriage has changed since they've become a Christian, and what helped them to change.
* Talk about specific ways you can grow to become more like Christ in your marriage.

Things to Do If You Want to Grow
* Write down one specific thing that you already know your spouse would love for you to change in your marriage role, and make a 40-day commitment to change it completely.

References for Further Bible Study
Genesis 2:18-25, 3:1-21 • I Peter 3:1-7 • I Corinthians 13:1-13 • Ephesians 5

Additional Resources
The Quiver by Douglas and Vicki Jacoby
Love and Respect by Dr. Emerson Eggerichs
His Needs, Her Needs by Willard F. Harley, Jr.
Created to Be His Help Meet by Debi Pearl
A Gentle and Quiet Spirit by Virginia Lefler
Love and War, Wild at Heart and Captivating (3 different books) by John and Stasi Eldredge

For additional resources or to join our online community, go to:
http://fieldguide.faith21.org

40

Parenting
Respecting Our Children

> *Fathers, do not exasperate your children. Instead,*
> *bring them up in the training and instruction of the Lord.*
> **Ephesians 6:4**

There are pivotal moments in our lives as parents that are etched in our brains forever. One of mine is a call from my son's third-grade teacher after his second day of school. Upon hearing her voice, my heart pounded loudly, while my nervous mind raced. "What could she possibly be calling about?" I argued in silent defense, bracing myself for the worst. After waiting for a few of the longest seconds of my life, his teacher spoke. "I just wanted to tell you that I've enjoyed getting to know your son during these first days of school. He's a very special person." I was a bit stunned. Until that day, no one had ever referred to any of my children as a "person." A kid? Yes. Been called a boy, a student, or even a rug-rat, but a real living and breathing separate PERSON? Never! Those words of appreciation from my son's teacher encapsulate my conviction about raising children. These precious miracle gifts from God (Psalm 127:3) are individuals worthy of R-E-S-P-E-C-T.

Many parents today are far too "busy," and often become irritated by their children's erratic or emotional behavior. Have you ever witnessed a parent chatting away on his cell phone while neglecting a simple, repetitious question from his child? Frustrated from trying in vain to get the parent's attention, the child becomes obnoxious. God, however, commands parents to not exasperate their children (Ephesians 6:4). How about the parent conducting business during a family outing? Not only have I witnessed these acts, to my shame, I've committed them myself. It is not difficult to imagine how children on the receiving end of neglectful parenting begin to see themselves as low priorities. Learning to respect our children's needs is relatively simple. In order to better understand this, we can count on the Bible for help. We often hear or preach about the need for husbands to feel respected by their wives, and for wives to feel loved by their husbands (Ephesians 5:22-33). Yet we are surprisingly slow in connecting to the fact that these little people also desperately need the same, to feel heard and understood. Love and respect are essential ingredients in the recipe of raising stable, confident, productive children.

Parenting can be the toughest job in the world, but when done right, it carries innumerable benefits. God desires that we excel in everything (II Corinthians 8:7). This is crucial when it comes to parenting. Though he was not a biological father, Jesus' example still inspires hope.

The call of parents is to give emotionally beyond their perceived ability. Paul commended the Macedonian church in II Corinthians 8:2-3 for a monetary offering exceeding their actual ability. Is giving emotionally any different? Our children face daily battering from a world that is always poised to rob their tender hearts of a desire for God or anything resembling faith. They experience a variety of growing pains during each season of their lives. Puberty is especially challenging. The changes during this time can be so frequent and dramatic that many a freaked-out parent has been known to think their child possessed! Consider the astounding patience, empathy and compassion of Jesus with Legion (Mark 5:1-20) and Mary Magdalene (Luke 8:2). They really were possessed. Despite their frightening behavior, Jesus looked past their actions and took the time to love them. This treatment ultimately won their lifelong love and devotion. Mary Magdalene couldn't bear a separation from Jesus (John 20:1-19). Legion begged to follow him (Mark 5:18). Love, respect and attention invested in your children will also inspire devotion and obedience from your child. This same devotion and obedience can be transferred toward Christ for the rest of their lives.

Do we assume things about our children or draw conclusions before we have all the information? Imagine yourself arriving home from an errand only to find your child playing a game or watching television. You specifically said to finish homework first. Since you've only been gone for an hour, there's no way could that homework be done. You proceed to correct and rebuke your child. At the end of your discourse, your child presents their neatly completed homework. Do you explain your actions away to save face, or accept that you were wrong and disrespectful and humbly apologize?

Do we entrust our kids and give them responsibility that is within reason for their age? At five or six, your child may begin to take on the chore of making his bed. Of course, it will not be picture perfect, nor should it be. They're kindergartners! Do you redo the bed, smoothing away the unevenness, or lovingly enjoy the sight of their lumpy bed and applaud their beginning efforts? If we are always fixing what our children do, we're sending them a message that they just don't measure up, that something is wrong with them. They'll soon lose their enthusiasm for responsibility without parental encouragement for completing their tasks.

We're very busy as parents, but it's vital to take the time to listen to our children's stories as they talk about their day. For example, your teenager sits nearby, weary and anxious, talking about challenges at his high school. But with the room to tidy up, dinner to prepare and calls to return, you multi-task distractedly, continually asking him to repeat himself. He soon leaves the room with an attitude. Is it surprising that your teenager felt disrespected when everyday chores couldn't be held for the time it would take to listen to his concerns? Unfortunately, he's likely to seek someone else who'll listen, and it could be a person with ignoble motives. When even bigger issues arise in your child's life, you may not be the first to know. So remember James 1:19: be quick to listen!

You may have been expecting a chapter about how to best discipline your children, and teaching them the fear of the Lord. Without a doubt, these are vital responsibilities (Deuteronomy 6:4-7; Proverbs 13:24). While loving your children, remember the importance of respecting them. Regarding respect, Romans 13:7 says to give everyone what you owe them. This includes children. Parental success will only come when we continue to follow Jesus' example of love and respect.

PARENTING: Respecting Our Children

Stuff to Talk Through With a Friend
* How can I show respect to my child?
* What can I do to give them individual time?
* Where have I been considerate and respectful toward my child?
* In what ways have I been disrespectful toward my child?
* Do I owe my child any apologies?

Things to Do If You Want to Grow
* Pray for humility to hear correction in the area of parenting.
* Ask other parents, including singles with or without children, for parental ideas.
* Set aside a regular, special time for just you and your child. Keep this time a priority.
* Notice your body language in speaking with your child. Look them in the eye when speaking. Stoop down to their level to address them. Offer gentle, reassuring touches when communicating during tough times.

References for Further Bible Study
Proverbs 22:6, 29:15-17 • Matthew 18:2-6 • Colossians 3:21 • James 1:19-21 • I Peter 2:17

Additional Resources
To Train Up a Child by Michael & Debi Pearl
Shepherding a Child's Heart by Ted Tripp
Raising Awesome Families in Troubled Times-Reloaded by Sam & Geri Laing
The Five Love Languages of Children and *The Five Love Languages of Teenagers* by Gary Chapman and Ross Campbell
But What About the Children? by Lee Boger
The Tender Years by Geri Laing and Elizabeth Laing Thompson

For additional resources or to join our online community, go to:
http://fieldguide.faith21.org

Section Four
Sharing the Light

The following twelve chapters will help any new believer understand some of the challenges of sharing Jesus with an unbelieving world. Some chapters will explain specific viewpoints of the world around us and others simply encourage us to be about the business of moving people toward Christ.

> *...so that you may be blameless and harmless, faultless children of God, living in a warped and diseased age, and shining like lights in a dark world.*
>
> Philippians 2:15 (J.B. Phillips)

41

Evangelism
Fishing With a Purpose and a Plan

> *When Jesus saw two fishermen, Simon and his brother Andrew, casting their nets into the lake, he said to them, "Come follow me and I will make you fishers of men."*
> Mark 1:17-19

Depending on your experiences when sharing your faith, Jesus' promise to "make you fishers of men" will evoke various reactions. You may simply think nothing could be easier than fishing for those interested in becoming Christians. Or, the very idea of fishing may conjure up fearful images of hanging on for dear life as your sinking boat is engulfed by one last monster wave. Even worse, you may believe that becoming a fisher of men might involve the most terrifying of all scenarios—public speaking!

Whatever your experience has been, Jesus has a promise for you. If you obey the calling of Jesus to "come follow me" and respond to the first promise he made to the disciples of "I will make you fishers of men," then you are on your way to fulfilling the greatest of all the commandments, to love God with everything in you and love others as you love yourself (Mark 12:30-31). By responding in obedience to Jesus' challenge, you are not only showing your love for God (John 14:15), but also a genuine faith in Jesus. The Bible speaks of genuine faith being that faith which is coupled with action (Acts 26:16; Matthew 22:39). So we see that both commandments can be fulfilled simultaneously; love God with your heart mind and soul, and love your neighbor as yourself. In the words of Paul Little, author of the classic *How to Give Away Your Faith*, "you must first have genuine faith to give away."

A speaker at a recent event recounted how he caught his prized Cordova fish, an impressive fish story that nearly rivaled Captain Ahab's pursuit of the White Whale. We all cheered; there is great satisfaction in outsmarting a fish with an IQ of 2.0. Our heroic fisherman had the proof to back up his story—a photograph posing with his beautifully eye-bulging trophy fish. You know, the kind of fish you can be proud to be seen with in public. It was definitely worthy to be mounted on a wall to keep any painting of Elvis in good company. Now, I regard myself a capable fisherman, so after his speech ended, I tracked him down and expressed my congratulations, from one fisherman to another, for such a fine catch. He was glad to talk more about fishing and seemed pleased that I too must be a member of the exclusive Fish Frying Fraternity.

However, in spite of my convincing enthusiasm for fishing, he surprised me with a most absurd question: "Are you a fisherman?" he asked. "Am I a fisherman?" I responded. "Of course I am a fisherman," I thought. Was he suspicious that I was not truly a member of FFF? Maybe it was that I didn't have a picture of me posing with my trophy fish, but it was obvious that he lost interest in speaking with me any further. Or maybe it was because I didn't have a fishing license or that I didn't have my own pole, fishing tackle box or fishing anything. Actually, the only fish posing going on was me posing as a fisherman.

In reality, I can only remember actually being successful at catching a fish once at Troutdale where you catch a fish in their pond (or your money back), and the other time fishing 50 feet downstream from a fish hatchery (which I think is illegal). So now I realize to my horror that, not only am I not a genuine fisherman, but I am really only a cheating fish stealer.

So then we should all take a closer look at what it means to be a fisher of men. Maybe you need some new ideas for your tackle box. For the Christian, a well-stocked tackle box means that you are fully equipped for every good work (II Timothy 2:15, 3:16-17). If you follow these tips, you could turn out to be a successful fisherman, rather than just a fishy philosopher.

First, build a list of friends and acquaintances and get to know them well. By knowing what concerns your friends, you can know how to pray for them and also know how to better serve them and spiritually meet their needs (Matthew 20:28). Treat people as unique and special. You may find someone who would not be interested in coming to church but would appreciate meeting for coffee and having their questions answered. Maybe your church offers a class they would be interested in. Discover what questions your friends may have and consider how to point them to Jesus. Ask questions and seek to understand more than to be understood. And remember that anything personal you learn from your friendship must be treated with absolute confidentiality. To be trustworthy is a hallmark of a good friend.

Don't get distracted with secondary issues. The most important issue is someone establishing a relationship with God through Christ. Don't let something they are doing destroy their opportunity to learn of the love of God. Whatever it is that offends you (their language, lifestyle, dress, beliefs or habits), it is secondary to them acting on the gospel (John 8:5-7;

Luke 11:46). You are welcome to rearrange the deck chairs on the sinking ship after God has repaired the giant hole in its hull.

Remember that the miracle of someone actually responding to the Gospel and becoming a Christian has comparably little to do with you. It has more to do with the Holy Spirit drawing on a person's heart (John 6:44). You are simply planting seeds of faith and it is God who multiplies your efforts (I Corinthians 3:7).

Through all of this, do not forget to develop a loving relationship with your God. Meditate on the word and the works of God. You may discover his works, both great and small, are expressions of his love for his creation, and his love should be your primary motivation for sharing the gospel. God's love must be at the heart of the gospel we offer to others (I Corinthians 13:1). The only thing that counts is faith expressing itself through love. Whatever approach you take to deliver the gospel, it should demonstrate God's love (Galatians 5:6). May God bless your efforts!

EVANGELISM:
Fishing With a Purpose and a Plan

Stuff to Talk Through With a Friend
* How often am I going about my business of fishing for men?
* What areas or situations are ideal for me to share my faith, and what areas or situations are challenges to me?
* Does my daily life show that I love God and love others?

Things to Do If You Want to Grow
* Find someone to coach you. If you can find a willing mentor to disclose how they achieved their success, then it may just be a matter of duplicating their efforts. Inspiring mentors, whether at church or even in a book or video, are ready to teach you how to share your faith more effectively. You can add your style to whatever method you like and make it your own.
* Build friendships with your brothers and sisters and discover exactly how they became Christians. You will be amazed at how God attracts people from all kinds of backgrounds and beliefs to Christ. Also, by having deeper friendships, you will know who would be best suited to help you reach out to a specific friend. Perhaps they both share an interest or may have even suffered a similar loss.

References for Further Bible Study
Acts 26:16 • Mark 8:38 • II Corinthians 5:20 • Matthew 28:19-20 • Acts 8:30 • Philemon 1:6

Additional Resources
How to Give Away Your Faith by Paul E. Little
Know What You Believe by Paul E. Little
Holy Conversation by Richard Peace
True and Reasonable by Douglas Jacoby
The Mission of God by Christopher J. H. Wright
Out of the Salt Shaker & Into the World by Rebecca Manley Pippert
The Man from George Street on www.youtube.com
Shining Like Stars by Douglas Jacoby

For additional resources or to join our online community, go to:
http://fieldguide.faith21.org

42

Shining Like Stars
And if You Must, Use Words

> *Religion that God our Father accepts as pure and faultless is this: to look after orphans and widows in their distress and to keep oneself from being polluted by the world.*
>
> James 1:27

The Bible teaches that God is greatly pleased with your decision to become a Christian (Luke 15:7; Psalm 80:3; II Thessalonians 2:13), and he wants you to pass on your life-changing conversion experience to others. But advocacy for Christ as the only road to God often leads to labels of "intolerance" or stern opposition to proselytizing. So how do we impact others in this age of political correctness?

As young believers, we may want to shout "I am a disciple of Jesus!" from the rooftops. There is nothing wrong with that level of passion. God recognizes such a declaration as honorable. However, most people will hear what you have to say better when they see you living the story you wish to tell. In other words, when your life shows "disciple of Christ" is when interest really perks up.

Jesus gives us a training ground to practice the actions of love in our own backyard—the Church. Jesus taught that "all people will know you are my disciples if you love one another" (John 13:34-35). Essentially, his premise indicates that telling people about love is far less effective in winning them over than actual demonstrations of love. Active love must become the defining characteristic of a disciple.

Because it is an action, love must be cultivated and practiced. Asking us to begin with our brothers and sisters in Christ is God's way of meeting us where we are. Tucked safely in God's family, we can learn the actions of love and become the people God intends us to be.

Though we may understand that genuine love is an action, many of us still subconsciously think of love as a feeling toward another person. It is true that you can have loving feelings for someone without actually loving them. For example, if a single mom you know is having a hard time financially and you happen to know she isn't able to put food on her table, it would be easy to mistake feeling sorrow for her (especially if that sorrow is accompanied by prayer that God will "be with her") as loving her. While compassion and prayer is a start, it is not the end of love where God is concerned (James 4:17). If on the other hand you showed up at her home with three or four bags of groceries or a gift card to a local grocery store, then that is love as defined in the Bible (see I Corinthians 13:4-7). The action of providing for her need will show her genuine Christ-like love, and those who see your actions will recognize that you belong to the family of God (I John 3:10).

Lifelong conditioning to our "me and mine first" culture makes it nearly impossible for many of us to take feelings and change them into action. Thankfully, however, the same day that your past sins were forgiven was the day that you started your new life; God gave you the gift of the Holy Spirit. One of the main purposes of the Holy Spirit is to transform us into the likeness of Christ, who showed us what real love is. Being transformed into his image is the only hope we have of truly living a life that attracts people to him.

The Holy Spirit will work on us, but we also must take action to help him in the process. One of the most basic yet most critical things we must do in order to be transformed into the likeness of Christ is read and study our Bible daily. When we examine the scriptures daily (Acts 17:11), the Holy Spirit prompts us to compare our thoughts, words and actions with the Word of God. Where they don't match up is where change can be initiated. When we obey God's Word, the Holy Spirit produces fruit in our lives. This fruit is the character of Jesus, the one whose image we are being transformed into. Reading, praying over, and obeying God's Word brings the transformation Jesus wants for us.

The actual transformation involves the process of transitioning our mind from being primarily concerned about self, referred to in the Bible as the sinful nature, to the mind of Christ, which is controlled by the Spirit (Romans 8:6-8). We must understand that the war between flesh and spirit will wage as long as we have flesh.

As in any war, battles will be won by both sides. However, the Holy Spirit gives us the power to win over the sinful nature. Saturating our mind with God's Word, and putting into practice to the best of our ability that which we have absorbed from Scripture, counteract the sinful desire of the flesh, through the power of the Holy Spirit. We hand the Spirit of God authority in our lives through our choice to obey his Word. The more victories are won over the flesh, the greater our transformation into the image of the Son of God.

A practical way to apply this principle is to use Christ's analogy of a fully-armed, strong man guarding his house and keeping his possessions safe (Luke 11:21). Which part of us is concerned with houses and possessions? Clearly it is the flesh, our sinful nature. Our flesh is a strong man because we've lived by it and let it control us most of our lives.

But there is hope. Jesus goes on to say that when someone stronger attacks and overpowers that strong man, he takes away the armor in which the man trusted (Luke 11:22). Think of the stronger man in the latter part of this story as the spirit who is strengthened through obedience to God's Word.

The more we set our minds on heavenly things, the more our words, thoughts and actions will reflect this change. Our lives will be a beacon that need no words to lead others out of darkness and into his wonderful light. Of course, our mouths must be a part of the transformation we go through as well. Just as Jesus was never afraid to speak the truth, so we will not let fear stop us from sharing our faith and the reason for the hope that is in us.

> *"Go out and preach the gospel, and if you must, use words."*
> **Attributed to St. Francis of Assisi**

When our deeds are consistent with our words, people, especially those who really know us, will be impacted greatly. So if you must, use words. But remember that your actions will always speak louder than any words you use.

SHINING LIKE STARS: And If You Must, Use Words

Stuff to Talk Through With a Friend
* What in your life reflects God's love?
* What in your life definitely does not reflect God's love?
* What in God's Word do you find hard to obey?
* What hinders daily study of God's Word?

Things to Do If You Want to Grow
* A detailed study and contemplation of I Corinthians 13:4-13.
* Pray for practical ways for reflecting this kind of love to others.
* Study how the Holy Spirit is transforming you into the likeness of Christ.
* Begin looking for ways to put into practice at least one thing from your daily readings.

References for Further Bible Study
Mark 8:34-38 • Luke 14:26, 14:33 • John 1:4, 8:31-32, 15:5-8 • Ephesians 4:22-24 • Colossians 3:9-10 • II Peter 3:18

Additional Resources
Discipling: God's Plan To Train and Transform His People by Gordon Ferguson
Growing True Disciples: New Strategies for Producing Genuine Followers of Christ by Georgia Barna
Becoming a Contagious Christian by Bill Hybells and Mark Mittelberg
The Unexpected Adventure by Lee Strobel and Mark Mittelberg

For additional resources or to join our online community, go to:
http://fieldguide.faith21.org

43

Respecting Authority
As unto the Lord

> *…there is no authority except that which God has established.*
> *The authorities that*
> *exist have been established by God.*
> **Romans 13:1**

The culture we live in has a "love/hate" relationship with authority.

On the one hand, we crave authority. In an age of the endless news cycle, there are countless opportunities to spy on what the politicians in power are doing. Daytime television is overrun by reality courtroom shows, with stern authority figures like Judge Judy being the most popular. Ask little children what they want to be when they grow up, and you will likely find the majority wanting to become some sort of authority figure, such as a policeman, firefighter or doctor.

On the other hand, we are bent on rebelling against authority. As much as we fixate on the power of politicians, we get a rush from being anti-establishment. If we are part of a worker's union, we're ready to strike as soon as management makes a decision that we don't like. If we're caught speeding, we're not apt to gladly accept the ticket; rather, we will experience a rebellious anger against the cop wielding his authority to penalize us for breaking the traffic laws. And what teenager naturally honors and respects his parents' authority? Christians must develop a proper understanding of and respect for authority because, as Paul teaches in Roman 13:1, "there is no authority except that which God has established." As creator of all authority, God is the authority figure over all things. If we rebel against the authorities God has established, we essentially rebel against God himself.

As Christians, we have a call to follow Jesus' Great Commission. At the end of his sojourn on Earth, Jesus told his disciples, "All authority in heaven and on earth has been given to me" (Matthew 28:18). Within his final teaching to his followers, Jesus conveyed to them that God had placed universal authority on him. Consider this assertion for a moment. This means that everything in the spiritual and earthly realms—from the angels in heaven to the smallest newborn baby—falls under the authority of Jesus Christ. He governs the rich and the powerful; the poor and the weak. He extends grace to both the holiest saint and the most wretched sinner.

The concept that Jesus is the ultimate authority must refocus our perception of authority. The apostle Paul writes, "He who rebels against the authority is rebelling against what God has instituted, and those who do so will bring judgment on themselves" (Romans 13:2). Biblically, our rebellion is not strictly limited to those human beings who are above us, but such rebellion is also directed at God himself. Take, for example, the authority wielded by the government in levying taxes, whether or not they are legally authorized to do so. Some would argue that Christians should not pay taxes as this money only supports the ungodly, political establishment. But when Jesus was confronted with the question of whether his disciples should pay taxes to the non-religious authorities, which in his case was the oppressive Roman Empire, Jesus shocked the crowd by indicating that his followers should render unto the secular authorities that which they demanded (Mark 12:17). By submitting to taxation, Jesus willingly humbled himself before the human authorities that God had established, thereby demonstrating his limitless respect for God's authority, despite the fact that the human authorities were misusing their power.

There is no biblical requirement for Christians to be doormats. However, our hearts need to be humble and willing to submit to the established authorities. We may disagree with or even dislike the people to whom God has delegated authority; however, it is ungodly to harbor rebellion against them in our hearts. In such cases, Paul's advice is this: "I urge, then, first of all, that requests, prayers, intercession and thanksgiving be made for everyone—for kings and all those in authority, that we may live peaceful and quiet lives in all godliness and holiness" (I Timothy 2:1-4).

In my life, rebellion against authority has produced more trouble than good. As a youth, whenever I rebelled against my parents, I created hurt and damage in our relationship that took many apologies, over the course of many years, to heal. When I was in my mid-twenties, I was diagnosed with clinical depression and was prescribed a therapeutic and medication regimen to address the problem. Because I was rebellious at heart, I thought that I knew better about my condition than my doctors, so I ignored their directives...which led shortly thereafter after to a terrible bout of near-suicidal depression and panic attacks, which took two years of treatment to overcome. Even as an older man, many years into my walk with Christ, I rebelled against the sound counsel of my trusted financial advisor, the consequences of which will likely follow me for years to come.

None of us is immune to such rebellion. All of us have some authority over us, and we are all tempted to push back, lash out, avoid or ignore such authority. Paul writes in I Peter 2:13-17, "Submit yourselves for the Lord's sake to every authority instituted among men: whether to the king, as the supreme authority, or to governors, who are sent by him to punish those who do wrong and to commend those who do right. For it is God's will that by doing good you should silence the ignorant talk of foolish men. Live as free men, but do not use your freedom as a cover-up for evil; live as servants of God. Show proper respect to everyone: Love the brotherhood of believers, fear God, honor the king." God will honor us for such a heart, and will provide us with the spiritual strength to respect the authorities he has placed in our lives.

As you interact with the authority figures in your life, further consider the following biblical principles:

* God says that if we rebel against authority, we bring judgment upon ourselves. In Romans 13, Paul explains, "Everyone must submit himself to the governing authorities, for there is no authority except that which God has established. The authorities that exist have been established by God. Consequently, he who rebels against the authority is rebelling against what God has instituted, and those who do so will bring judgment on themselves."
* Follow the example of Jesus. Submission and rebellion are polar opposites. In Philippians 2:5-11, Jesus submitted himself to the unjust authority of the Pharisees and the Romans to be crucified. Although he is omnipotent, Jesus allowed himself to be sacrificed on our behalf. It is Christ-like for us to imitate such humble obedience.
* In church, the recognized leaders have a high calling in

conjunction with their authority. While we may not agree with them on every point of theology and ministry, Hebrews 13:17 exhorts us to "Obey your leaders and submit to their authority. They keep watch over you as men who must give an account. Obey them so that their work will be a joy, not a burden, for that would be of no advantage to you."

RESPECTING AUTHORITY:
As unto the Lord

Stuff to Talk Through With a Friend
* What is the quality of working relationship with your superiors at work? Do you feel comfortable being subordinate to your employer?
* When you hear a teaching at church that does not make sense or with which you disagree, what kinds of internal reactions do you experience?
* Describe your feelings when you think of the government, church leaders, police officers and doctors. What you feel about these types of people will give you insight into the quality of your respect for authority.

Things to Do If You Want to Grow
* Decide that you will be a peacemaker rather than a rabble-rouser. Anyone can complain and stir up trouble. Very few people can humbly accept a position with less authority than their neighbor without getting agitated.
* Accept a belief system that God actually created. Authorities on Earth are for our benefit.
* Remember that human authority is fallible, but to disrespect human authority is to disrespect the ultimate authority—God himself.

References for Further Bible Study
Daniel 7:13-14 • II Corinthians 10:1-8 • Ephesians 5:21-33 • Colossians 2:8-10, 3:18-23 • II Peter 2:9-13

Additional Resources
Business by the Book by Larry Burkett

For additional resources or to join our online community, go to:
http://fieldguide.faith21.org

44

Excellence at Work
God Is Your Boss

> *Whatever you do, work at it with all your heart, as working for the Lord, not for men, since you know that you will receive an inheritance from the Lord as a reward. It is the Lord Christ you are serving.*
> **Colossians 3:23-24**

Do you ever find yourself bragging about your job or your amazing boss? Have you ever found yourself telling anyone who will listen about your very understanding, charismatic, forgiving, nurturing and inspiring supervisor? If that is the case, you probably are in the very small minority of all employees in the world. For most of us, the perfect boss is as elusive as winning the lottery.

Take comfort...Joseph did not start out well either; talk about a less-than-perfect first interview: "Meanwhile, the Midianites sold Joseph in Egypt to Potiphar, one of Pharaoh's officials, the captain of the guard" (Genesis 37:36). However, this did not stop Joseph from being the best employee he could be. Since Joseph put God first, he experienced success in everything he did (Genesis 39:5).

Being excellent at work is a decision that you must make regardless of how your boss treats you (Colossians 3:23-24). Even though Joseph did everything right in his job, he still ended up wrongfully terminated. Unlike today, Joseph had no option to bring legal action against Potiphar; instead, like a Monopoly player with bad luck, he was sent directly to jail for his alleged poor job performance. Nevertheless, it was all in God's plan. Because of his faithfulness to God, not only did Joseph get out of jail, but he ended up becoming the second in command in the country of Egypt. Talk about getting promoted!

The boss you have at work now is the boss God intended you to have at the present time to help you with your character. You may think you have the worst employer and the worst job ever, and you cannot wait to quit. As hard as it may be, God has a plan in this, "because we know that suffering produces perseverance; perseverance, character; and character, hope" (Romans 5:3-4).

Laws now differ greatly from those in Joseph's time. You probably will not end up in jail if you leave your job, and chances are no employer wants to deal with a wrongful termination lawsuit. Most employers want to give annual reviews, some even do quarterly reviews. Most of us get a paycheck on time every time. Most of us know that if we do the bare minimum at work, and do not get in much trouble, we may get a "cost of living" increase every year and that is fine. Nevertheless, that is far from being excellent and what God called us to do as Christians. God calls us to be the best at our work. In America, there is a growing phenomenon called the "entitlement trend." In fact, lots of employees nowadays feel their bosses owe them for just showing up to work.

Much research has been done in corporate America about employee motivation and work performance, leading to the development of a whole new industry called "Performance Management." Corporations in America are consumed with getting their employees to be the best that they can be. This may seem novel to many of us, but "Be All You Can Be" was not the recruiting slogan of the United States Army for over twenty years without good reason. Your earthly boss could change everything in the work environment, from increasing your pay to changing the light fixtures, with the intent to help you be productive and excellent at your work, but if the desire to be excellent does not grow from within you, no such measures will work. The motivation to be excellent does not come from the environment, but from within, and the truth is excellence takes hard work and commitment. There is a reason why so many scriptures talk about the value of hard work (Proverbs 18:9, 21:25, 31:17).

I have devoted the last few years of my life to working in the field of behavior management for kids with autism. In this arena, the most successful parents are the ones who exhibit the greatest motivation to do whatever it takes to help their children change their socially inappropriate behaviors into effective ones, even when their children have limited skills to help themselves. Talk about courage to help their kids be excellent! Being a parent is hard, but being a parent of a child with autism is much harder. For these parents, excellence is simply defined as having the kids who exhibit typical child behaviors.

Being excellent takes courage and playing by the rules—for the Christian, by God's rules. I grew up in El Salvador, a third-world country, in the middle of a civil war. I knew early in life that I had no choice but to be excellent if I was ever to accomplish anything. Being mediocre meant being drafted in the army against my will, and I did not want that. I remember my parents telling me the only inheritance they would give me was going to be an education, and that was it. So growing up, my motto became "If it was going to be, it was up to me." By the grace of God, I was able to come to the United States on a Fulbright Scholarship based on my academic achievements. When I started working after college, I became obsessed with being the best at work. When things were going my way, I was okay with following the rules, but when things were not, I was tempted to cheat the system to achieve my goals. I knew deep inside that it was not right (I Samuel 8:3; Amos 8:5). When I became a Christian, I was convicted by the examples of my heroes in the Bible, especially Joseph. Joseph did not get a great start and had every excuse not to be excellent, but he was nonetheless. The story of Joseph is one that inspires me every day. Joseph did it against all odds and he ended up saving the nation of Israel.

Here are some tips to help you with excellence at work:

* Make a decision in your heart that God is your boss at work. Regardless of the way your boss treats you, God has given him to you for a reason, so learn the lesson that God has for you (Colossians 3:23-2).
* Learn to take constructive criticism and advice well from your boss and your superiors, for that is the beginning of wisdom (Proverbs 12:15, 13:10, 19:20, 20:18).
* Do not compromise your Christian values for the love of money. All of us want to be successful in our careers and be recognized for our work. However, the sin of greed lurks nearby. Avoid greed at all cost. No sin can shatter your career path more than green. Be open about your temptations in this area, "For the love of money is a root of all kinds of evil. Some people, eager for money, have wandered from the faith and pierced themselves with many griefs" (I Timothy 6:10).

EXCELLENCE AT WORK:
God Is Your Boss

Stuff to Talk Through With a Friend
* Are you finding any areas in which you are compromising your integrity at work?
* Are you dealing with greed at work? If so, what can you do to deal with it?
* How was your last annual evaluation? Was that something to be proud of? If not, what must you do to earn a great review next time?
* How is being excellent for you defined at your work?
* Would you hire yourself if you were your boss?

Things to Do If You Want to Grow
* Stop being mediocre and decide you will be the best employee your employer ever had.
* What kind of additional education would you need to become better at work? Are you pursuing it?
* Find a Christian mentor in the business world, preferably in the same industry that you are in, and ask him/her to coach you for six months and hold you accountable to your own goals.

References for Further Bible Study
Genesis 2:15 • Psalm 90:17 • Proverbs 14:4, 14:23, 18:9, 21:25, 22:29, 31:17

Additional Resources
Business by the Book by Larry Burkett

For additional resources or to join our online community, go to:
http://fieldguide.faith21.org

45

Relatability

Understanding and Reaching Those Around Us

> *Though I am free and belong to no man, I make myself a slave to everyone, to win as many as possible.*
> **I Corinthians 9:19-22**

Churches are full of all kinds of people. There are the wealthy who don't have a material care in the world, and right next to them are those who are mere days away from living on the street. There are people who have spent years in prison, and those who have never even gotten a speeding ticket. There are people who love their hip-hop music (the Wal-Mart versions, of course), and there are others whose iPods have nothing but Garth Brooks and Sara Evans on them. There are Conservatives and Liberals and members of every race under the sun. There are surfers, CEOs, teenagers and widows.

At some point in the lives of these people, they heard and responded to the common call to discipleship, but, as they took upon themselves Jesus' Great Commission, they quickly realized that the rest of the world was full of people with whom they could not easily relate. Throughout the Bible, Christians are exhorted to learn to relate with others in order to win them to Christ, and a proper understanding of that is crucial for winning the world.

We call this phenomenon "relatability," and its most famous biblical expression comes from the Apostle Paul in I Corinthians 9:19-22. Sometimes, there is a temptation to read this passage and take away from it a general call to learn what our non-Christian friends like to do and go do those things with them. We will go to jazz clubs with jazz fans and go golfing with avid golfers, even if we don't get jazz and cannot golf. (Speaking only for myself, if you are lousy at billiards, I would just as soon not play with you.) Surely the sentiment is appreciated, and it is important to do whatever you can to build great friendships with people. But, the teaching in this scripture has broader implications than simply joining non-Christians in activities they like.

In this famous passage, Paul begins by saying that he makes himself a "slave to everyone." Paul's implication is that as a spiritual slave to Christ, he chose to make himself a slave to everyone else as a way of reaching them for Christ. In humbling himself to people of all kinds, Paul sought to relate to people in whatever station of life he found them. By doing so, he became a servant to their spiritual needs, just as Jesus did during his ministry.

Thereafter, Paul describes his attitude toward several groups of people: those with and without the law, the Jews and the weak. We rarely contemplate people in these ways. We tend to differentiate people by gender, economic status and race. These differences are arbitrary and, ultimately in God's economy, unimportant. The differences Paul is talking about require learning and understanding. What does it mean that one person is "under the law" while another does not have the law? Who are the weak? What does that mean? Considering the full scope of this teaching, it is fair to postulate that those under the law are not only people with a belief in the Bible. It would also be insufficient then to decide that those without the law are those without a Christian tradition. It is biblically inaccurate to conclude that the weak are solely those who are struggling in their faith.

If we apply these concepts to the modern world, those under the law are people who believe that there really is truth and that life has meaning. They believe that God has determined the high and low, the noble and ignoble, right and wrong. Those not having the law will often see the world as hopeless and meaningless. For them, morality is relative, and relationships have no foundation. A person's life is nothing but an idiosyncrasy in a world of nihilism.

In considering how the Christian church should be compassionate toward the Jews, we must understand that Paul was talking from both a personal and global perspective, as a person of Jewish ethnicity who had adopted the Christian faith. Also, the context in which Paul was writing was that Christians were a small sect compared to the vast Jewish community, so his was a virtually inaudible voice among a chorus of well-known singers. Today, the opposite is true: Christians far outnumber Jews in the world, so our voices are loud compared to the relatively slight sound of the Jewish community. When we consider the weak, our first response is to offer compassion, but often, what they really need is our strength. Compassion without responsibility harms people (II Thessalonians 3:10). All of this is to say that relatability ought not to be confused with being like other people or doing the things they like to do. It means understanding other people.

If there is one thing that is clear in the New Testament, it is that God likes to turn man's wisdom inside out. God had Paul the Pharisee and Peter the uneducated fisherman at his disposal. Man's wisdom would have counseled that Paul would be the perfect apostle to the Jews. Who could be more relatable to them than a converted Pharisee? Peter appears to have been a more relatable choice to minister to the Gentiles, and his friendship with Jesus would surely have helped them to overcome their unbelief. God did the opposite. He sent the Pharisee to the Gentiles and the fisherman to the Jews.

It is easy to reach out to someone like you, but how do you know that God has not chosen you to bring the gospel to another person specifically because you are complete opposites? Those are the times when God's power is most plainly seen, that God is the one at work. It is when we believe that the poor can save the rich, and the healthy can save the sick, and the young can save the old, and the Nigerian farmer can save the Portuguese merchant that we come to understand an important aspect of Christ and the gospel.

What we need to understand is that everyone is first and foremost a spiritual being, and no one can be properly understood as an isolated individual. As Jesus chose to share in our humanity (Hebrews 2:14), we share in the humanity of those around us. We are not merely individuals with common biology; we are mothers, sons, brothers, daughters and citizens, all of which define us in our relationship to other people. God has called us into his perfect family, of his choosing, not ours. Understanding where we come from means recognizing what separates us is nothing compared to what we share in common.

So relatable or not to another person, as ambassadors of Christ, we are called to reconcile people to God, despite the differences that keep people divided from each other and from him.

RELATABILITY:
Understanding and Reaching Those Around Us

Stuff to Talk Through With a Friend
* Do you have close friendships with people who are not like you? Do you find it difficult to be close to people who do not appreciate your culture or background?
* When you meet someone who is not like you, is your first thought that you need to introduce him or her to a person with whom they would share a lot in common? Why?
* When was the last time you went out of your way to learn about other cultures and other ways of life?

Things to Do If You Want to Grow
* Walk up to a person you have nothing in common with and learn something about them. Don't just invite them to church, investigate who they are.
* Research a religion or an ethnicity you know nothing about, then find someone of that group and strike up a conversation.

References for Further Bible Study
II Corinthians 5:11-20 • Galatians 2:6-10

Additional Resources
A Farewell to Alms by Gregory Clark
The Quest for Cosmic Justice by Thomas Sowell

For additional resources or to join our online community, go to:
http://fieldguide.faith21.org

CHRISTIAN CONUNDRUMS

War

Not surprisingly, war has always been a dividing subject. Should a Christian engage in violence against an enemy? Throughout the centuries, this question has been answered by Christians in very different ways. Following are the two extremes; Christians usually fall somewhere in the middle:

Only in Certain Situations

This viewpoint allows that we are called to love our enemies, but states we are also instructed to take care of our own families. Before Jesus went to the cross, he made sure that his followers had swords to defend themselves. He never would have wanted us to allow evil to triumph over us or other people in need. We are put here to fight against injustice and oppression—sometimes that involves the sword. God encouraged his people to war in certain situations in the Old Testament, and the same is true today.

Never

This viewpoint allows that war was condoned in the Old Testament, but Jesus changed everything. We, as Christians, are to live as Jesus lived. He spoke out against oppression, sometimes forcefully, but he never took up the sword for any cause. Though he could have destroyed his enemies with a word, he did not defend himself against any of their cruelty. We, as Jesus, are to be peacemakers and never engage in violence, even in self-defense. We must follow Jesus' command to love our enemies and pray for those who persecute us.

Seek justice, encourage the oppressed ...
Love your enemies, do good to those who hate you
Luke 6:27, Isaiah 1:17

46

Firestorm!
Persecution in Our New Lives

> *"In this world you will have trouble.
> But take heart! I have overcome the world."*
> John 16:33

Wouldn't it be nice if after you were baptized your family showered you with congratulations, your old friends started singing "Hallelujah," your boss immediately understood your request to have every Sunday off and your neighbors decided that next week they would start coming to church? Ideally, everyone you know should treat your baptism as a celebration on Earth just as there was rejoicing in Heaven at your conversion (Luke 15:7-10). The reality is, however, that while God is ecstatic that you have chosen to follow Christ, the people with whom you share this earthly life are often apathetic, callous or downright nasty about the fact that you are no longer diving headfirst into the reckless lifestyle of sin in which they continue to immerse themselves (I Peter 4:4). For this reason, Jesus himself tells us that the world will offer trouble to his followers...but to his praise and glory, Jesus delivers us!

The opposition you may face regarding your conversion to Christ is a biblical phenomenon called persecution. In varying degrees throughout church history, Christ's disciples have experienced all kinds of obstacles caused by people who disagreed with the Gospel. While this is an unpleasant reality, the Bible forewarns Christians that we need to be prepared to face such opposition. In his last known correspondence, the Apostle Paul told his apprentice, Timothy, that "everyone who wants to live a godly life in Christ Jesus will be persecuted" (II Timothy 3:12). Although persecution is unwanted, we should not be surprised when it occurs. In fact, if we respond to persecution faithfully and courageously, we will find "that the testing of [our] faith" will develop our "perseverance"; and if we develop perseverance in the face of persecution, we will become "mature and complete, not lacking anything" (James 1:2-4).

We can consider ourselves fortunate that God has blessed us to live in a time when Christianity is relatively acceptable and in a society which offers much protection against persecution. In biblical times, Christians often faced fierce opposition, including imprisonment, physical suffering and even the death sentence at the hands of the established religious and political authorities of the time. Even today, there are places in the world where sharing the gospel is illegal, where the Bible is banned and where conversion to Christianity is a capital crime. In fact, nearly 200,000 Christians are killed worldwide each year because of violent persecution! Those of us who live in free societies, therefore, must rejoice that we can follow Christ with little concern that we will be treated as criminals for our faith.

There are forms of persecution in our society that are not violent, but which still threaten our relationship with God.

As a new disciple, you are likely to find yourself at odds with those closest to you when you show them the degree of participation with which you have in attending church, which is one way that you demonstrate your commitment to God. When I was converted, I told my friends that I no longer had as much free time to spend in frivolous activities because I was involved with Sunday worship, Tuesday midweek service and time with my Bible study group. The general response to my devotion was, "What are you doing all that for?" One friend of mine who practiced a different form of Christianity gave me a bunch of negative literature to read, the content of which was skewed to indicate that I didn't need to follow the Bible literally and that my newfound commitment to Christ was excessive. Interestingly, this same friend had never shared his faith with me or urged me to read the Bible prior to my conversion. Because I am ethnically Jewish, one of my co-workers, who is also Jewish, insulted me by saying that my conversion to Christianity made me a traitor to my fellow Jews. Also, it took my physical family several years to stop badgering me with questions like, "How can you possibly believe the Bible? It's all myth!" and "Why do you need a religious crutch to get on with life?"

None of these insults threatened my physical well-being, but they were forms of persecution, and they certainly shook my faith. As a new Christian whose roots in God were just developing, my faith could have been stifled when my family, friends, and co-workers put such obstacles in my way. By the grace of God and the love I had for the Bible, I was prompted to immerse myself in the Word. I also had close relationships in the church to reinforce my roots so that I could withstand the persecution. In the same way, you are likely to experience opposition in your walk with Christ. You may undergo insults or jokes at your expense because of your faith. Some friends or family may not wish to associate with you as before because they see you now as a "Jesus-freak." Perhaps your employer will give you all kinds of grief because you are not as available to work any and every shift due to your new church schedule. The persecution you experience may be more severe than what I've gone through, and I pray for you that it will be less. In either case, I encourage you to gird yourself with the Bible and in the fellowship so that you can hold yourself close to Christ, with deep roots in him as Lord and Savior.

Practically speaking, here are some tips to help you withstand persecution:

* Strengthen your own convictions with scriptural wisdom. God teaches us that knowledge and understanding of his Word produce faith (Romans 10:17). You can discern between fact and fiction more readily when you have a good working knowledge of the Bible.
* Be as prepared as possible for potential persecution as a spiritual reality (Hebrews 10:33; Revelation 2:10). Recognize that Jesus himself anticipated and underwent persecution, so as his follower, it is likely that to some degree you too will experience persecution (John 15:20).
* Anchor yourself to a small group of believers (Hebrews 10:25) for encouragement and support when you are undergoing persecution. Remember Ecclesiastes 4:12—there is strength in numbers.
* Persecution never feels good, nor would anyone want to experience it. Nonetheless, our great God sent Jesus—who acknowledged that we would have trouble in this world—to provide the power to overcome it!

FIRESTORM!
Persecution in Our New Lives

Stuff to Talk Through With a Friend
* What type of persecution are you seeing in your life?
* What are you learning and how are you growing through persecution?
* Do you expect your Christian life to be easy or hard? Why?
* How does this expectation affect your outlook on life?
* How does knowing you are not alone in suffering persecution make you feel?

Things to Do If You Want to Grow
* Stop complaining about persecution and start thanking God on a daily basis for the things he is teaching you.
* Encourage a brother or sister who is going through a hard time. Listen to them, and, if they are open to it, share with them what you have learned.
* Research ways that you might be able to help Christians around the world who are under intense persecution. Choose to do something definite to help.

References for Further Bible Study
Psalm 9:13-14, 119:84-88 • Matthew 5:10, 5:23, 13:18-23, 24:5-13 • Acts 13:32-52 • Romans 8:35 • I Corinthians 4:10-13 • I Thessalonians 3:6-7

Additional Resources
Because They Hate by Brigitte Gabriel
Tortured for Christ by Richard Wurmbrand
Christian Persecution Worldwide (www.youtube.com)

For additional resources or to join our online community, go to:
http://fieldguide.faith21.org

47

Other Churches
Are We Alone in Our Christianity?

> *"I have other sheep that are not of this sheep pen. I must bring them also. They too will listen to my voice, and there shall be one flock and one shepherd."*
> John 10:16

The New Testament indicates that part of Jesus' mission was to establish the church among his followers. Yet the definition of "church" is one of those critical items given to us in the Bible that is not explicitly defined. The English word church comes from the original Greek New Testament word ekklesia, meaning "assembly of citizens summoned by the crier." But church is more than that. We are told how, at conversion, God grants us his Holy Spirit, empowering us to live a Christian life and adding us to the body of the church. Groups of people with the Holy Spirit are singularly called "the church," both locally and as a worldwide community (Acts 18:22; Ephesians 3:10).

In order to understand the biblical nature of the church, we need to search the Bible for its distinctive qualities. Accordingly to Acts 2:42-42, God's church, of which Jesus is the head (Matthew 16:18; Colossians 1:18), must be devoted to the scriptures, relationships with other Christians, communion in remembrance of Jesus (the breaking of bread) and prayer. God also expects accountability in his church (Matthew 18:15-17; Galatians 2:11); confronting sin is a part of being devoted to the scriptures.

Membership in the church is reserved for true Christians, or disciples of Christ. A Christian does not become one by being born into a Christian family or nation; becoming a Christian is a voluntary act (Matthew 28:18-20; Mark 1:16-20). In fact, in the *New International Version* (NIV) Bible, the word "Christian" appears just three times (Acts 11:26, 26:28; I Peter 4:16). However, the word the Bible uses hundreds of times for a personal follower of Jesus is "disciple." This was even Jesus' word of choice and it retains a sacred association (Matthew 10:42; Mark 14:14). The term "Christian" was first used in Antioch, the Syrian capital, explicitly tagging Jesus' followers, who were busy causing trouble all over the world (Acts 17:6-7)! Christian is now the more popular term, but if we consider its biblical origin, we should consider it synonymous with disciple.

Many other attributes of a disciple, who is a member of the church, are given throughout scripture. A disciple of Jesus...
* Believes and obeys (John 4:50, 8:31)
* Studies and applies the scriptures (Luke 6:47-48; Acts 17:10)
* Helps others become disciples (John 1:42; Acts 4:20, 18:24-25; Philemon 6)
* Keeps growing spiritually (Colossians 1:10; II Thessalonians 1:3)
* Serves others (Mark 10:45; Acts 9:36)
* Is 100% committed to God (Matthew 6:33; Luke 9:62)
* Voluntarily confesses his sin to other disciples (James 5:16)
* Loves deeply and unconditionally (Matthew 5:44; John 13:12-13)
* Has a balanced yet full life (John 10:10)

* Displays humility to the utmost (Philippians 2:5; John 6:64-66)
* Has surrendered the control of his life (Luke 14:25-33)

All of the above qualities are visible in the daily lives of genuine, biblical Christians, as those around us will attest. These qualities are so well defined that even unbelievers are able to readily judge who is and who is not a Christian (Acts 19:15)!

To our shame, one of the problems that has constantly plagued the Church is a lack of unity. Believe it or not, complete spiritual unity is possible; Jesus prayed for it in John 17:20-23. Unfortunately, instead of unity, we have century-old denominationalism. Our sin has divided what began as one church, separated only by distance, into thousands of disassociated groups called denominations. These autonomous churches teach their own brand of doctrine based on various understandings of the Bible. Paul rejoiced when the Corinthian Church repented of this type of division (I Corinthians 1:10-13; II Corinthians 7:8-11).

The causes for the separation of God's church in the modern day into various denominations and groups within those larger denominations are many. The main reason is a two-thousand-year conglomeration of rules taught by men, as opposed to a strict adherence to the Bible (Mark 7:7; Colossians 2:8). Unfortunately, the one teaching that divides us most is also one teaching where no one can afford to be wrong: the teaching on salvation.

The major division among Christians involves a myriad of Catholic, Orthodox and Protestant churches. The first two major denominations, Catholic and Orthodox, generally teach that salvation happens at baptism, including infant baptism. Most Protestant denominations such as Anabaptist, Anglican, Assembly of God, Baptist, Episcopal, Lutheran, Methodist,

Presbyterian and other smaller churches typically believe that baptism is merely a symbol, or ceremony, of the salvation that has already taken place at the time of an individual's belief in Christ as Savior. Further division between these Protestant denominations happens in smaller groups. Some groups believe that only faith is necessary for salvation, others believe that repentance and discipleship, making Jesus the Lord of your life, is also necessary. On one extreme, some groups go so far as to say that all you need to do is ask Jesus to "come into your heart" in order to be saved. On the opposite spectrum, some more legalistic groups teach that you must also obey the Law of Moses to be saved. Most churches fall somewhere in the middle.

One major Protestant denomination, the Church of Christ, teaches that salvation includes faith, repentance and making Jesus the Lord of your life. Our family of churches descends directly from this denomination, and also we believe the Bible is very clear on these issues. Like them, we believe the Bible teaches that when a person of age makes a choice to follow Christ and be baptized, that baptism is the point of salvation.

In addition to these beliefs which we share with our brothers and sisters in the Church of Christ at large, our particular family of churches also holds to a position that discipleship to Christ is a necessity for salvation. In our view, a Christian has the same definition as a disciple of Jesus. Our contention from the Bible is that you cannot say that you are a Christian, a Christ-follower, if you do not follow Jesus Christ.

No matter the church, one problem a young Christian will have is walking the line between pride and confusion. On the one hand, you will have the temptation to be judgmental toward other Christians based on their beliefs. On the other hand, you will be tempted to throw your beliefs out of the window and accept everybody as a believer. Pray that you are able to remain faithful in what you believe the Bible teaches while accepting others who are living as Christians and yet may believe differently than you do (Luke 11:23; John 13:35; Romans 14:4).

In summary, God designed church as a community of believers who worship in truth (John 4:23). This is the kind of church that Christians should seek, through prayer and comparison to the church modeled in Acts 2:42-47. Anticipate imperfection; you are there! Even so, the best investment you can make is fellowship with like-minded, heart-bonded Christians. There's no place like God's home (Ephesians 2:19)!

OTHER CHURCHES:
Are We Alone in Our Christianity?

Stuff to Talk Through With a Friend
* What was your church experience growing up? How does it differ from your current discipleship experience?
* Do you currently attend a church matching the description of Acts 2:42-47?
* If not, are you willing to pray about connecting to one?

Things to Do If You Want to Grow
* Look over the list of a disciple's attributes above and write down the ones you think you are weakest in. Then ask a friend which ones you need to work on. Compare both answers and make a decision to work on one of your weaknesses.
* Have conversations with Christians from other denominations. Note the areas they are similar to your church, and the areas where they differ. If anything is lacking in their experience, share what you have at your church.

References for Further Bible Study
Acts 4:2-4, 4:32-35, 9:31 • I Corinthians 16:1-2 • II Corinthians 6:14-17, 8:1-5 • Ephesians 4:3-6 • I Thessalonians 1:1-10

Additional Resources
Foxe's Book of Martyrs by W. Grinton Berry
Complete Guide to Christian Denominations: Understanding the History, Beliefs, and Differences by Ron Rhodes
Handbook of Denominations 12th Edition by Frank S. Mead, Samuel S. Hill, Craig D. Atwood
The Kingdom of the Cults by Walter Martin

For additional resources or to join our online community, go to:
http://fieldguide.faith21.org

CHRISTIAN CONUNDRUMS
Politics

Modern Christians are divided politically. Each election season, leaders from all sides of the political spectrum claim to be *the logical choice* for people of faith. How can liberals and conservatives claim to be Christians and at the same time not be unified politically?

The secret is in the driving force behind politics: **the dream of changing the world for the better**. The difference between ideologies is not the dream; the difference is *how* to achieve the dream:

Liberals usually believe that the government has the *responsibility* to change whatever is wrong in our world. Poverty, unemployment, crime, lack of education, sickness, racism and oppression of any kind should be dealt with through government programs. It is also the job of government to enforce fairness throughout society in order for all people to have equal access to the benefits of modern society.

Conservatives usually believe that individuals and groups of individuals are responsible to change our world for the better. They tend to look at government and government programs as failures and actually the cause of many of the problems they intend to fix. Equality between people will be achieved through personal responsibility and hard work as long as there is little interference from the government.

Obviously, these are very broad strokes. The thing to remember is that both of these political leanings can be believed in by a Christian—the question is *which of them actually works*.

All of you, clothe yourselves with humility toward one another
I Peter 5:5

48

Moral Relativism
Do All Roads Lead to Rome?

> *You may think you are on the right road and still end up dead.*
> Proverbs 14:12 (CEV)

Everything is relative...or is it? Virtue can be described as character excellence derived from recognizing and embracing what is noble and true (Philippians 4:8). Moral relativism is a highly pervasive view in our society, advocating that moral and ethical standards are culturally based, and therefore subject to individual interpretation. Moral relativism, being unbound by absolute standards of any kind, says "It's true for me, if I believe it." Centuries ago, Pontius Pilate asked, "What is truth?" in order to sidestep personal responsibility in crucifying Jesus (John 18:38). This same argument is used today. Although it would seem this philosophy is a contemporary phenomenon, moral relativism has imposed an enduring and long-standing influence on American values. In 1848, celebrated author Charles Dickens offered this critique:

> *"The American elite is almost beyond redemption...Moral relativism has set in so deeply that the gilded classes have become incapable*

of discerning right from wrong. Everything can be explained away, especially by journalists. Life is one great moral mush—sophistry washed down with Chardonnay. The ordinary citizens, thank goodness, still adhere to absolutes...It is they who have saved the republic from creeping degradation while their 'betters' were derelict."[1]

Moral relativism may very well have a stronghold on some of our own thinking, even as Christians. Its many proclamations may sound or even feel right, but are completely wrong (Proverbs 14:12). The Bible teaches that God's thoughts and ways are superior to ours (Isaiah 55:8-9), cautioning us to avoid fine-sounding, spiritually deficient teaching (Colossians 2:8). Examine your own thought patterns and beliefs after reading this chapter.

As the effects of moral relativism have slowly diffused, impressionable youth are reaping the disturbing harvest of unprincipled seeds sown throughout our educational system. A recent poll indicated that 75% of American college professors currently teach there is no such thing as right and wrong. Queries regarding good and evil are considered "relative to individual values and cultural diversity."[2] In promoting this notion of "intellectual neutrality," moral absolutes are nullified. School condom distribution, campus violence, "sexting," teen pregnancy, and "baby daddies" have escalated in the wake of moral relativism. Regardless of parental outcries, California public school teachers legally teach and encourage sexual experimentation, beginning with junior high students. Classrooms are also being used as platforms to promote political homosexual agendas like gay marriage. Moral relativistic attempts to "normalize" homosexuality in America

---
1 Charles Dickens, *Dealings With The Firm Of Dombey And Son: Wholesale, Retail And For Exportation* (London: Bradbury & Evans, 1846-1848).
2 Zogby poll (2002).

are largely rejected, as evidenced by presently 30 states having passed constitutional laws defining marriage as God designed it in Genesis 2:20-24. California law requires strict proof of age 21 or over to purchase beer, yet a 12-year-old can legally obtain an abortion without parental knowledge or consent. Parental consent, however, is required to extract a minor child's tooth!

Mankind instinctively understands that moral absolutes exist (Romans 2:14-15). It is the reason we feel emotional and mental nudging when we've violated God's standards or even our own conscience. Consider that all cultures respect honesty, courage and wisdom, while denouncing lying, theft and murder. They may emphasize or define these values differently, but the differences are largely superficial. C.S. Lewis' simple yet brilliant observation puts it this way:

> "They [different cultures] have only had slightly different moralities. Think of a country where people were admired for running away in battle, or where a man felt proud for double-crossing all the people who had been kindest to him. You might just as well try to imagine a country where two and two made five. Selfishness has never been admired. Men have differed as to whether you should have one wife or four. But they have always agreed that you mustn't simply have any woman you liked."[3]

Consider one of the popular sentiments of moral relativism: "Who are we to judge what is right and wrong?" If someone were to state, "In my opinion, Elvis Presley is dead," can that person be both right and wrong? If Elvis is dead, then they are right; if Elvis is alive, then they are wrong. Although they might not know if they are right or wrong, they are either right or wrong since both statements cannot be true at the same time.

---

3   C.S. Lewis, quoted in J. Budziszewski, Written On The Heart: The case for natural law (Downer's Grove, IL: InterVarsity Press, 1997).

Proponents of moral relativism will even quote the Bible to back up their views: "Judge not, lest ye be judged!" This quote from Jesus in Matthew 7:1 usually doesn't arise unless one's morals are being scrutinized. As in the case of Pilate's "what is truth?," "judge not, lest ye be judged" has been used as an escapist opportunity to deny moral absolutes. The twisting of scripture is one of Satan's favorite pastimes, and this example has contributed to the dissolution of the family unit in our modern society. Scripture clearly states the sinful, injurious nature of sex outside of marriage (Ephesians 5:3; Hebrews 13:4), and yet "non-judgmental" moral relativism obscures the clear directive. Of course, once the moral relativistic proposition was accepted, it became "sex is all right if we're engaged" and then, "it's all right if we love each other" and finally, "it's all right—period." In the end, moral relativism asserts that anything we do is acceptable and gives false worth to "grey" areas of behavior. God's truth and moral relativistic reasoning cannot both be true.

We free and empower ourselves by adhering to II Corinthians 10:5, taking captive the thoughts of the world and making them obedient to Christ. All created things are subject to a set of laws, whether natural laws like gravity or divine. Our actions definitely matter—both now and for eternity. Let the world know there is absolute truth that is not up for debate.

MORAL RELATIVISM: Do All Roads Lead To Rome?

Stuff to Talk Through With a Friend
* Has moral relativism influenced your faith?
* Do you believe God has established moral absolutes?
* Can faith in God and moral relativism co-exist?
* Can one's faith still grow if God's values are not fully embraced?
* Does God accept all people as they are?
* Does it really matter what YOU believe about God and the Bible?

Things to Do If You Want to Grow
* Pray for God to reveal moral relativism in your thinking and beliefs.
* Pray about scriptures you may "disagree" with.
* Make your own list of common moral relativistic questions and prepare yourself with biblical answers.

References for Further Bible Study
Judges 17:6, 21:25 • Psalm 139:24 • Jeremiah 5:30-31 • Hosea 4:1 • Luke 14:34-35 • II Corinthians 10:12 • Colossians 4:2-6

Additional Resources
True for You but Not for Me by Paul Copan
Relativism: Feet Firmly Planted in Mid-Air by Francis J. Beckwith, Gregory Koukl
Prepared to Answer: Restoring Truth in an Age of Relativism by Gordon Ferguson

For additional resources or to join our online community, go to:
http://fieldguide.faith21.org

49

Humanism
Does Man Control His Own Destiny?

> *The Lord knows the thoughts of man; he knows that they are futile.*
> Psalm 94:11

It could be argued that most of the modern world's inhabitants are humanists, whether they admit it or not. As Christians, we must understand what humanism is so that we can reach out to the humanists we run into on a daily basis and help them understand true Christianity.

Humanism is a replacement for religion, and is even recognized as a legal religion in some countries. Humanists would rather describe their beliefs as a lifestance: what you accept as true and of ultimate importance, which you commit to and practice living out.[1] However, no two humanists are exactly the same. Humanism is a peculiarly flexible belief system that adapts to almost every personal situation. If we want to help humanists to know God, we need to understand the underlying beliefs that support their lifestance.

At the core, humanism does not allow a traditional belief

---

1 From the entry for "Life Stance" in Wikipedia.org

in God. One of the central truths of humanism is that only science can prove truth; and because God cannot be proven through scientific methods, he either does not exist or is entirely irrelevant to our lives. In no way does he have an effect on the universe or on individuals. If God did exist, humanism asserts it would be impossible to know him, in the same way an ant could never know and understand a human being.[2]

A few years ago, I was at an impasse in a discussion with a humanist, a common occurrence. When all of my arguments for the existence of God were either ignored or summarily rejected, I finally asked him, "Could it be that you do not want to accept the existence of God because if you did, you know you would have to obey him?" After a short pause, he answered and admitted that to be true. You see, for a humanist, morality does not come from God or a sacred book. In fact, there are no universal moral laws. Ethics and morals are believed to have evolved with man and discerning right and wrong in a particular situation can only be done through the intellect. As long as you can rationally explain your actions to yourself, you have not violated your ethical standard. This belief is obviously very convenient since it can be used to justify ANY type of lifestyle or belief; however, humanism is not necessarily an easy way to live.

Humanists strongly believe that all of man's problems can be solved by man alone. The goal of a humanist is to find fulfillment and happiness in making the world a better place. Working together as mankind toward a better world is the true humanist's vision. In fact, the failure of religion to eradicate the world's many problems is the stated reason for the birth of modern humanism as stated in the first Humanist Manifesto

---

2 *All references of humanist beliefs come from the four major Humanist Manifestos which can be found in many different locations on the internet.*

of 1933. If we as Christians had been living God's light in this world, there would never have been an excuse for humanism.

Another basic tenant of humanism is that humanism itself will evolve. There is no universal truth; therefore humanism itself changes from year to year. Humanist manifestos have been written and signed by many of the leading humanists in the world (1933, 1973, 2000 and 2003). Each of these documents interestingly notes the flaws in previous versions. For example, after the devastation of the Nazis in World War II, the 1973 version had to recognize that science could be used for evil, as well as good. To be fair, the overarching goal of making the world a better place has stood the test of time, though exactly how to do it changes from generation to generation.

More recently, humanists have come to grips with the fact that a spiritual dimension is needed in our lives in order to give us meaning. To meet this need, the Law of Attraction was born through huge media successes like The Secret.[3] This humanistic idea adds an element of spiritual purpose (without God) to the lives of people who otherwise look for purpose only in the physical, visible world.

The dangers of humanism are many. First of all, everything starts with man instead of God. The need for a savior is categorically denied because man is not sinful and can, in fact, solve all of his own problems. Because there is no absolute moral code, sins like abortion, euthanasia, suicide, sexual aberrations, pornography, prostitution, adultery and divorce can be necessary and even good depending on the situation. If the baby would be unloved, it is kind to kill her. If grandmother cannot take care of herself and is in pain, terminating her is actually an act of mercy. Even horribly destructive sins can be

---

3 *The Power of Positive Thinking* by Norman Vincent Peale in 1952 was a precursor to what is being so effectively re-packaged today.

explained away when the standard of absolute good and evil is denied. As Christians, we must confront these beliefs with the truth of God's Word.

The first and primary step in reaching out to humanists is to simply live the life of a disciple of Jesus. Our Savior taught that the greatest commandment, after loving God, is to "Love your neighbor as yourself" (Matthew 22:39). Throughout the Bible, we are commanded to take care of the poor and the needy around us, which is the only religion that God accepts (James 1:27). Of course, we don't want to do good deeds for the praise of men, but Jesus says "let your light shine before men, that they may see your good deeds and praise your Father in heaven" (Matthew 5:16). Remember, our lives should be our calling card when visiting a humanist.

Only after displaying God's work in our lives are we ready to discuss the intellectual arguments of humanism. One of the major difficulties you will encounter is that most humanists consider themselves to be intellectually superior and look at religious people as irrational. Never pretend to have all the answers; humanists respect seekers. Begin by asking questions about their beliefs and follow it up with tougher questions that make them think.

Sadly, humanism exists in part because of our failure to live like Christ. Try to never argue with a humanist (II Timothy 2:23). Rather, show them your life and then ask them questions. Be prepared to share the hope that is in you by your actions and words (I Peter 3:15).

HUMANISM: Does Man Control His Own Destiny?

Stuff to Talk Through With a Friend
* Have I been influenced by humanist thinking?
* What types of humanist influence can we see around us? What can we do about it?
* Is my life an example that displays true religion for all to see?

Things to Do If You Want to Grow
* Find two or three ways to live your life in service to the poor and needy outside of church. Dedicate yourself to serving in these areas consistently.
* Read all four major Humanist Manifestos.
* Become familiar with advanced questions for a humanist and be ready to ask them. Following are a few examples you could use:
* You say that God cannot be proven through science. What are the empirical scientific tests that could prove the existence of God? Who decided what these tests should be?
* You say that you can only be sure of truth that you can prove logically. How can you prove that logic is the basis for discovering truth?
* Where did logic come from? (It could not have evolved because it would not be logic if it was not 100% logical.)
* Logic is abstract or nonmaterial, applicable to everything or universal, invariant because it never changes, and external to the whole universe. Where did it come from?
* Can you accurately observe laws and principles in the universe? If so, why? (Saying that it is because of those same laws and principles is circular reasoning.)
* What is the cause of everything? Keep asking "and what is the cause of that?" until they arrive at the unknown point.

References for Further Bible Study
I Timothy 5:4 • Amos 8:4-10 • Deuteronomy 15:11 • Proverbs 14:31 • Romans 1:20 • I Corinthians 2:14, 3:20 • II Corinthians 10:5 • Acts 17:24-28

HUMANISM:
Does Man Control His Own Destiny? cont...

Additional Resources
Is Man The Measure? An Evaluation of Contemporary Humanism by Norman Geisler
Relativism: Feet Firmly Planted in Mid-Air by Francis J. Beckwith, Gregory Koukl
How Should We Then Live? The Rise and Decline of Western Thought and Culture by Francis A Schaeffer
American Humanist Association (www.americanhumanist.org)

50

Atheism
Does God Exist?

> *The fool says in his heart, "There is no God."*
> Psalm 14:1

Immanuel Kant once said, "It is wisdom that has the merit of selecting, from among innumerable problems that present themselves, those whose solution is important to humankind." The most important of these problems is the existence of God. Everything else follows from it. How should I live? What is right and wrong? Does life have any meaning? What is praiseworthy and what is blameworthy? Do the True and the Good really exist? The answers to these questions are completely different depending on whether or not one believes God to exist. The first part of this chapter makes the case that God does exist, but the second part is probably more important for the average reader. It deals with the question of whether or not God exists for you.

The idea that science and religion are at war with one another is debatable. These disciplines have different functions; they can be complementary. Science is concerned with description, while religion is concerned with prescription. The scientist can create weapons of war, but without morality of some sort (generally predicated on a religious value system), he is utterly incapable of telling us when to use them. Likewise, a chemist might seek the benefit of his minister's biblical discernment to learn how to apply his laboratory skills in a righteous manner, yet he probably wouldn't ask his minister to describe the difference between covalent and ionic bonds. Science and religion often seem to be in competition because they both claim to seek the Truth and they are both engaged in the same battle: to overcome Nature. The truth is, the more science discovers, the stronger the evidence becomes that God does, in fact, exist.

It would be impossible in the space of one short chapter to enumerate all of the different ways that science continues to affirm the existence of God, but let us consider two compelling examples: the Big Bang Theory and the Anthropic Principle. The Big Bang Theory is often proffered as the scientific alternative to the Genesis story, but many cosmologists and theoretical physicists are uncomfortable with it because they understand its unavoidable consequences. If the theory is correct, then there was a Beginning. That may seem obvious to us today, but that was a radical claim for the Book of Genesis to make. To the human observer, the universe appears fixed, constant and static. It wasn't until the 20th century that science was able to recognize what the Bible had claimed for thousands of years. Science does not like ultimate beginnings because every effect requires a cause. What caused the Big Bang? Many brilliant scientists have spent decades trying to come up with theories that don't require a first cause, but the evidence keeps getting in the way.

The Anthropic Principle is the recognition that the entire

universe is governed by laws that seem designed with human life in mind. Consider the following:

* If the rate of expansion one second after the Big Bang had been smaller by even one part in a one hundred quadrillion, the universe would have recollapsed upon itself.[1]
* Known universal constants exist, such as the strong nuclear force and gravity, which govern the universe. Change any one of them and life cannot exist. The odds of all of these being precisely what they need to be for life to exist: one chance out of, well, the number doesn't have a name. It would be a one followed by 229 zeros.

In the world of science, a chance that miniscule is considered mathematically zero. So, how do atheists get around this near impossibility? They postulate infinite universes. They suggest that there may be parallel universes, or even that the current universe is just the latest iteration of a universe that expands and contracts infinitely. Is there evidence for these hypotheses? No. But, the atheist recognizes that while a one followed by 229 zeros is a very large number, it is just a drop in the bucket compared to infinity. By imagining infinite universes, he can turn a mathematical impossibility into a mathematical certainty. At this point, however, the atheist has put his hope in an infinite number of unobservable worlds, whereas the Christian has put his hope in just one such world. To complicate matters further, the atheist has only succeeded in engineering a universe where life is possible. The leap from non-living matter to living matter in that hard-won universe is just as improbable. Then we have an almost unbelievable leap from simple life one day, to life that is capable of reproducing itself the next. And then, the leap from living matter with reproductive capability

---

[1] Stephen Hawking, *A Brief History of Time* (New York: Bantam Books, 1996), 126.

to sentient, self-aware beings is another equally unlikely event. Given this scientific evidence, no rational person could deny the existence of a Designer.

In the 1880s, Friedrich Nietzsche famously declared "God is dead." He didn't mean that there was no god. He was getting at something much more profound. He was saying that no one takes God seriously anymore. For all intents and purposes, God has no relevance in people's lives. They claim to believe in him, but, in our religious vernacular, they don't make him Lord. The world is full of such people. Here are two indicators that God is dead for you:

* If your relationship with God is entirely private and personal. God is not your buddy. He is not that happy voice in your head telling you that you are "special," and that the most important thing is to be "true to yourself." You need to be true to him, and he is public.
* If you think of yourself as a "white person," a "woman," a "minority," an "American," etc., before you think of yourself as a Christian. We used to be "foreigners and aliens." We used to be "Jews, Greek, slave [and] free." Now, we are members of God's household, brothers and sisters with a common Father.

If we do not take God seriously, he may as well not exist. He needs to frame every aspect of our lives. He has determined what is right and wrong, and we need to conform our minds to his. Without God, your life is meaningless. With God, your life has terrific meaning, but that meaning comes from the will of God, not from your will. God wants everyone to be saved and to come to a knowledge of the truth (I Timothy 2:4). That means you need to proclaim him in every part of your life. Let us show the world that God not only exists: he is ALIVE.

ATHEISM:
Does God Exist?

Stuff to Talk Through With a Friend
* If there is no God, where does morality come from? Does your idea of morality consist of more than just compassion for the weak against the strong? If so, what are some examples? If not, why not?
* How can one believe in an omnipotent, omniscient, benevolent God in a world full of evil and suffering?
* Can you demonstrate that the God of the Old Testament is identical to the God of the New Testament?

Things to Do If You Want to Grow
* Learn to love God with your mind. It is not enough that you accept the existence of God as an article of religious faith. Do not concede the ground of reason to the atheist. His task of substantiating his belief is much more difficult than yours. And, confront your atheist friends with the necessary, unavoidable consequences of their beliefs. Without God, there is no right and wrong, there are no such things as individual rights (which include his right to freedom of conscience), and there is no justification for the equality of all people. If you are not familiar with these arguments, learn them.

References for Further Bible Study
Job 26:6-14 • Psalm 14:1 (The Hebrew words rendered fool in Psalms denote one who is morally deficient.) • Romans 1:20 • Romans 8:19-22 (The Anthropic Principle)

Additional Resources
What's So Great About Christianity by Dinesh D'Souza
There Is a God: How the World's Most Notorious Atheist Changed His Mind by Antony Flew, Roy Abraham Varghese
Republic by Plato (The second most important and influential book in history after the Bible)
Is There A God? by John M. Oakes
The Resurrection: A Historical Analysis by Foster Stanback

For additional resources or to join our online community, go to:
http://fieldguide.faith21.org

51

Science and the Bible
Where Do We Come From?

Do you not know? Have you not heard? The Lord is the everlasting God, the Creator of the ends of the earth.
Isaiah 40:28a

Every public school in America teaches Darwinian Evolution, which can be defined as genetic changes in organisms from one generation to the next. Over time, these small changes accumulate and can cause substantial differences, even leading to new species. Similarity among species suggests that all known forms of life descend from a common ancestor.[1] This theory has become the standard explanation for the origin of life on this planet. Darwinian Evolution is, figuratively speaking, in the DNA of most books, television shows and movies, and is only disbelieved by religious fanatics, or so we are told.

In fact, microevolution, or changes within a species, is not being questioned. Most, if not all, scientists believe that species evolve within their own species. The proposition before us is macroevolution: the evolution from one species to another. If

---
1 Paraphrased from the entry for "Evolution" in Wikipedia.org.

you move to Africa, chances are your great-grandchildren will be darker skinned than you are, but should you expect future generations to display characteristics of lions or elephants? Most Christian scientists would say that macroevolution is a myth—and thus would take a stand against Darwinian Evolution.

However, before we consider whether the Theory of Evolution is truly the explanation for life, we must first inquire about the origin of life and it's Creator. Who or what is the creator of everything we see around us in the world today?

The Bible clearly tells us that God is the origin of all life. He is the Creator of everything we see, and everything we don't see (Colossians 1:16). Whether he used evolution as a way to create or not is a secondary issue. We must not forget this basic truth: God created everything, including you and me.

Most teachers of evolution, however, would say that the origin of life on this planet is not God, but rather random chance. The Theory of Evolution has an explanation for where most species came from; in reality, however, the explanations begin to crumble the farther back they attempt to reach. Rationalizing that a man came from a primitive man, who came from an ape, may sound plausible, but attempting to explain primordial soup giving life to the first organism is a lot more difficult. In fact, when asked the origin of the mysterious gases supposedly exploding in a Big Bang which jump-started life, most scientists will simply tell you that nobody knows.

So, immediately we are faced with two opposing propositions to explain the creation of life. One assertion points to God as the origin of life, and the other points to random chance, implying no known origin. Both of these beliefs are outside of provable science, therefore neither can be called "scientific." Unfortunately, the Theory of Evolution is commonly referred to as science while the biblical story of creation is commonly regarded as merely a religious perspective. The choice is really up to the individual whether he or she will believe the black robes of religion or the white robes of the scientist. While some people may strongly disagree with this point, it takes just as much blind faith to believe one theory as it does to believe the other. It is also understandable why many teachers of Darwinian Evolution are agnostics or atheists. What is the point of the existence of God if he is not the source of everything?

The shocking effects of our society choosing the Theory of Evolution as the explanation for life are plain to see. Adolph Hitler, Joseph Stalin, Margaret Sanger and other infamous 20th-century characters never doubted they were performing mankind a service by ridding us of the "less than human" people. For example, the ideas of Darwin were often quoted in Hitler's book *Mein Kampf* and were used to promote his agenda of exterminating Jews. Darwin himself prophesied that this would happen: "At some future period, not very distant as measured by centuries, the civilized races of man will almost certainly exterminate, and replace, the savage races throughout the world."[2] While genocide may be an extreme result, our society has embraced other less obvious products of this belief: abortion and euthanasia. If a baby is going to have a defect, why not kill it? If an old man can no longer take care of himself and is in pain, why not end his misery? These are the logical conclusions to a belief system that replaced God as the origin of life and forgot how precious it is to him (Romans 1:18-25).

Once we are clear on God being the origin of life, we can consider whether the Theory of Evolution is a truthful explanation of how life came to be. As Christians, one way of

---

2   Quoted from chapter 6 of *The Descent of Man* by Charles Darwin.

understanding the creation account in Genesis is God creating the world and all distinct species of life in six literal days. In this view, evolution is categorically dismissed. However, many Christians believe that the "days" from Genesis chapter one could refer to ages of time, not literal 24-hour days. In this view, evolution could hold some truth. Interestingly, both of these beliefs are based on different interpretations of the original Hebrew word for "day" as used in the first chapter of Genesis. Each Christian is advised to take a deeper look at these two possibilities and to take a stand for what you believe—a stand full of humility and grace. Remember that if you know all the right answers but fail in love, you have gained nothing (I Corinthians 13:2). On the other hand, make sure your stand is based on God's word, not on what may be more popular today.

In summary, never forget the primary question: who or what is the cause of our world? No matter what method God used to create the universe, it was still he who created it. It is still he who planned it perfectly for our use and set each of us to live in the exact time and space where he wanted us to be in order to reach out to him and find him (Acts 17:26-27).

SCIENCE AND THE BIBLE:
Where Do We Come From?

Stuff to Talk Through With a Friend
* Where do I get my beliefs on creation?
* Am I prepared to answer anyone who asks me the reason I believe in a Creator?

Things to Do If You Want to Grow
* Read a book and do research on the Theory of Intelligent Design.
* Ask other Christians what they believe about evolution and why.
* Research the different Christian stances on "old earth" vs. "young earth" science.

References for Further Bible Study
Genesis 1 & 2 • Exodus 20:11 • Romans 1:18-25 • Psalm 14:1, 53:1 • Proverbs 1:7 • Matthew 7:18

Additional Resources
The Privileged Planet DVD with John Rhys-Davies
Icons of Evolution DVD with Steve Meyer
Unlocking the Mystery of Life DVD with Jay Richards
Expelled: No Intelligence Allowed DVD with Ben Stein
The Case for a Creator by Lee Strobel
Secrets in Polar Ice by A. Watt and P. Hansen
The Source by John Clayton
Genesis, Science and History by Douglas Jacoby
Answers in Genesis: www.answersingenesis.org
Institute for Creation Research: www.icr.org
Science and the Bible by John M. Oakes
That You May Believe by John Oakes and David Eastman
Reasons For Belief by John M. Oakes

For additional resources or to join our online community, go to:
http://fieldguide.faith21.org

CHRISTIAN CONUNDRUMS
How Did We Get Here?

Besides dealing with the scientific theory of evolution, Christians have differing opinions among themselves as to when and how God created the universe and all life.

Young/New Earth Creationism

The universe, the Earth and life were created by God in a literal six days. All of creation is less than 10,000 years old. The dating of creation starts with the recorded time of King Saul, around 1020 BC, and counts backwards using the numbers given in scripture. The old look of the Earth is by design, to function correctly, just as Adam and Eve were created as adults. Creation science interprets discoveries in view of the literal interpretations of the Bible, such as the Flood as the cause of the extinction of dinosaurs.

Old Earth Creationism

The universe, the Earth and life were created by God, but not in a known time span. Current evolutionary dating of hundreds of millions of years is accepted as a reasonable span for creation. Macroevolution is possible, though unproven. There are three main old earth positions.
1. Gap Creation: the belief that God created the universe and the Earth, then waited an undetermined amount of time to begin creation of life.
2. Day-Age Creation: the belief that God created everything in a time span of his own time, not a literal one.
3. Progressive Creation: the belief that God has intervened in the creation of the universe, the Earth and life over time in specific critical stages.

In the beginning God created the heavens and the earth.
Genesis 1:1

52

Social Justice
And as You Read This...

> *The Spirit of the Sovereign LORD is on me, because the LORD has anointed me to preach good news to the poor. He has sent me to bind up the brokenhearted, to proclaim freedom for the captives and release from darkness for the prisoners.*
> Isaiah 61:1

As you read this, there is a need somewhere in the world that God can use you to fulfill. Yes, you, me and all of God's sons and daughters have been elected to affect positive social change: "You, my brothers, were called to be free. But do not use your freedom to indulge the sinful nature; rather, serve one another in love" (Galatians 5:13). Change, where an entity enters another state of being, is the goal. However, if we want to have an affect and bring good and lasting changes, we must be aware of the visible and invisible forces that influence the world around us.

Visibly, we witness that no matter how our economy fluctuates, our mainstream Western culture still advocates materialism, cheap sex, excessive money and chemical highs. We see anxious winners, depressed losers, more me-me-not-you-but-me-but-blame-you attitudes, less family, less community, less effective government, less church, less accountability, less forgiveness, less mentoring. We still experience a world of social, financial and educational marginalization.

World religions say our problems are the result of our sinful nature; psychology calls it our innate ego or our natural need for security—self-centeredness, really. Social critics say the radical individualism seen today reflects the price of living in a "free" world, yet most of the world's population lives in poverty. While all of this is visible to the careful observer, the invisible, spiritual reality mirrors the happenings in the world we see around us: "For our struggle is not against flesh and blood, but against the rulers, against the authorities, against the powers of this dark world and against the spiritual forces of evil in the heavenly realms" (Ephesians 6:12).

Considering the earthly and spiritual context of the mess we have made of our world, how does one engage social activism? How does an activist keep his head up in a time of discouragement, when all around us are needs nobody seems to be meeting? Here are some ways:

* Remember that what you do is for God's glory and not your own (Matthew 25:40).
* Be open to the fact that your goals may not always be his goals. However, if you trust him, you'll see that his outcome is more fruitful than you thought possible (II Corinthians 9:12-13).
* Multiply your prayer life. Not only ten-fold but fifteen-or more-fold! Don't underestimate the power of prayer. Even medical research shows that patients who are prayed for fare better than those who are not[1] (Psalm 66:20).
* Know that God wouldn't give you a bad end of the deal if you dedicate yourself to service. You won't lose yourself, but find greater confidence through Christ, prayers answered

---

1 http://www.ncbi.nlm.nih.gov/pubmed/3393937

before your own eyes, despair replaced by incredible joy and insecurity replaced by empowerment (Jeremiah 29:11).
* Know that someone is bound to persecute you for your faith or for the cause that God placed on your heart. But take it as a thumbs-up for doing something right for God (Romans 5:3-4).

What exactly can you do? God commissioned you to spread the gospel (Matthew 28), and one way to reach out to people and teach others to reflect his light is to fulfill a need (James 1:27). Instead of just waiting around for him to bless those in need, be a blessing. Some examples of projects that you could pursue:
* Spend a holiday together to re-paint a local school.
* Celebrate Valentine's Day at a local nursing home.
* Inform the community about the local threat of toxic waste.
* Purchase inexpensive laptops for children in rural or poor areas of the world, even in the US.
* Use a social online network to arrange a prayer marathon for struggling countries, for political and cultural leaders, or for the armed forces.
* Host an open-mic night to raise money for an orphanage or to pay for an expensive sonogram for a clinic in a poor neighborhood or poor country, so that more women will choose life.

Through you, God teaches others to not only be on the defense but also on the offense. "For if the trumpet give an uncertain sound, who shall prepare himself to the battle" (I Corinthians 14:8)? Recent examples of God's successful social projects include:
* The tiny church that filmed and produced "Fireproof" in 2008—turning an unheard of $500,000 budget into a $33 million profit, forcing Hollywood to respond instead of the

other way around.²
* Rick Warren and Saddleback Church building medical clinics in developing countries.³
* The International Churches of Christ, who even through years of growing pains and self-reflection, trusted God's powerful steps and continued providing millions annually to Hope worldwide.⁴
* The Los Angeles Christian Health Center becoming, in 2008, the first Christian-run, medical clinic offering a full range of free services to primarily homeless individuals and families.⁵

After more than two years of serving as medical social worker and psychotherapist with LA Christian Health Center, I now serve in the same capacity at a secular clinic with the JWCH Institute. The work can be very demanding, especially during tough economic times and lack of resources. More often than not, I work with other agencies that, despite their mission statements, are very bureaucratic and discouraging to those in need. If you said years ago, when I earned my Master's Degree at an Ivy-league school, that I would work in Skid Row, I would've told you "No way, I've worked too hard pulling my own bootstraps to end up down there." Yet, I love this work because God continues to use my experiences to minister to me, as well as reward me both professionally and financially in ways that I did not think was possible. The work gets even more exciting when I apply prayer to situations instead of feelings, and in turn witness God gracefully opening doors for my patients. In our current economic downturn, prayer also eased my worries when funding ended for my position

---

2 http://www.nytimes.com/2008/10/06/movies/06fire.html?_=1&scp=1&sq=%22Fireproof%22%20the%20film&st=cse
3 http://www.time.com/time/nation/article/0,8599,1830147-1,00.html
4 http://www.hopeww.org/NetCommunity/Page.aspx?pid=206
5 http://www.ladowntownnews.com/articles/2008/08/04/health2/health02.txt

with my previous employer. God answered with a new job at a nearby clinic and a huge pay increase! All things work for his glory (I Peter 4:11).

May you and those you serve witness God's power more and more through your volunteering or professional activism. The action he has for you awaits!

SOCIAL JUSTICE:
And as You Read This...

Stuff to Talk Through With a Friend
* Is there a need in the world that God can use you to fulfill?
* How are Christians called to affect positive social change?
* How can you best prepare yourself for social activism and times of discouragement?
* What are some projects that you can tackle with your church, family and community members?
* How is prayer a valuable tool for activists? What are other tools an activist can use and where does prayer rank among them?

References for Further Bible Study
Exodus 1:15-22 • Luke 10:25-37 • Mark 4:18-19 •
I Corinthians 12: 12-25 • Romans 8: 29-39 • James 1:27

Additional Resources
Jesus Wants to Save Christians by Rob Bell
The Irresistible Revolution by Shane Clairborne
The Mission edited by Randy & Kay McKean (Chapter: To Heal and to Bring Good News to the Poor by Bob & Pat Gempel & Mohan Nanjundan)
Desiring God by John Piper (Chapter 9, Missions: the Battle Cry of Christian Hedonism)

For additional resources or to join our online community, go to:
http://fieldguide.faith21.org

The Rest of the Journey

Dear Friend,

Congratulations! If you have followed my suggestions, you are a full year into this book. I trust that it has blessed you in the same way it has me.

Where do you go from here? Well, seek to walk with God in prayer and daily reading of his word. That is the first thing. Additionally, here is a list of books that every Christian should read (not in any particular order):

- The Pursuit of God by A.W. Tozer
- The Calvary Road by Roy Hession
- The Power of the Spirit by William Law
- Mere Christianity by C.S. Lewis
- Pilgrims Progress by John Bunyan
- Fathered by God by John Eldredge (for men)
- Help Meet by Debi Pearl (for married or soon-to-be married women)
- In His Steps by Charles Sheldon
- Knowing God by J. I. Packer
- More Than a Carpenter by Josh McDowell
- How to Read the Bible for All Its Worth by Gordon Fee
- Church History in Plain Language by Dr. Bruce Shelley

Put what you are learning into action and follow the prompting of the Holy Spirit in every area of your life where he shines the spotlight.

Finally, please join our community at http://fieldguide.faith21.org as we explore the Christian life together. I look forward to getting to know you.

"I am confident that he who began the good work in you, will be faithful to complete it and take you home with him one day."
Philippians 1:6 (J.B. Phillips)

With love in our common Lord,
An Anonymous Christian

AUTHOR BIOGRAPHIES - The Maturing Process

Adam Smith
4/27/2003
As a new Christian, Adam thought worship bands were totally lame. Today he leads a church in Bozeman, Montana, where he also plays guitar and leads worship songs to God.

Allen Pellerin
6/22/1982
As a new Christian, Allen was deeply moved that Jesus immediately lit a BBQ after his resurrection. Today he leads a Grief Recovery ministry and is still inspired by the loving nature of God.

Ben Valentin
7/25/2006
As a new Christian, Ben thought of church as a gas station, where you simply came to get filled up. Today he lives church 24/7, reaching out Jesus' hands to the poor and needy.

Christian Ray Flores
12/23/1995
As a new believer, Christian challenged a 285-pound mafia thug to be a "real man" and follow Jesus. Today he serves as an evangelist at Turning Point, and still challenges scary people.

Christopher Torres
4/30/1995
As a new Christian, Chris asked God for an Oscar for best actor. Today he no longer acts, but rather teaches financial stewardship God's way and serves on various financial and missions boards.

Curtis Reed
10/16/1994
As a new Christian, Curtis was just focused on landing a good wife. After 12 years of being single, he finally married and now preaches and leads the ministry for singles at Turning Point.

Dan Hagadorn
1/15/1995
As a new Christian, Dan was busted late-night-smoking by a big church leader. Today his breath is fresh as he serves in the Turning Point teaching ministry as well as Faith21.

Darlene Bel Grayson
4/28/1988
As a new Christian, Darlene was the only one who raised her hand when asked "who is worthy of eternal life?" Today she humbly writes for Faith21 and is a part of a new church planting.

AUTHOR BIOGRAPHIES - The Maturing Process

Deborah de Flores
4/19/1992
As a new Christian, Deb invaded a drinking party teaching about sin with Galatians 5:19-21. Today she teaches her daughters at home while serving in the full-time ministry at Turning Point.

Guy Hammond
8/15/1987
As a new Christian, Guy *knew* he would be a minister in a few day (it took 12 years!). Today he leads a church in Halifax and helps disciples with unwanted same-sex attractions (StrengthInWeakness.org).

James Bean
5/20/1990
As a new Christian, James gave his rent money in a special offering. Today he writes for Faith21 and serves in the financial ministry at Turning Point while still meeting his responsibilities at home.

James DonVito
9/23/2000
As a new Christian, James argued that the term "Priest" was not in the Bible. Today he uses his artistic talents for God as well as writing for Faith21 and FusionFilter.com.

James Sulewski
7/28/1991
As a new Christian, James rolled up to a church service at the park with his skateboard and no shirt. Today he dresses appropriately as he plays with the band and preaches at Turning Point.

Jamie Parker
1/28/1996
As a new Christian, Jamie achieved perfection and could not understand why others were so messed up. Today he has a masters in theology and realizes that he knows only God's grace.

Jason Baars
10/1/1998
As a new Christian, Jason was disruptive when anybody would try to teach a Bible lesson. Today he helps to lead pre-teens in his church and teaches parents how to raise Godly children.

Jay Minor
11/22/1993
As a new Christian, Jay wanted to skip a baptism so he could "be relatable" and watch X-Files with his neighbor. Today he is an evangelist at Turning Point and leads the family ministry.

AUTHOR BIOGRAPHIES - The Maturing Process

Jerry Gaona
10/18/1998

As a new Christian, Jerry tried to inspire a 13-year-old telling him that Jesus was baptized at 13. Today he is an example to all in evangelism and sharing God's love with accuracy.

John Steinreich
8/28/1994

As a new Christian, John stayed home during the holidays to legalistically not miss a midweek service. Today he writes for Faith21 and published "The Words of God?", a book on Islam and Christianity.

Jonas Walker
3/10/1996

As a new Christian, Jonas would often wear a shirt sporting a marijuana leaf. Today he serves in a chemical recovery group at Turning Point that helps others live without drugs and alcohol.

Joseph Dindinger
4/17/2000

As a new Christian, Joseph rejected other Christians who didn't agree with him. Today he serves God by leading the Faith21 ministry and helping believers grow in their faith.

Kim Upton
3/20/1987

As a new Christian, Kim burst into tears when unable to find biblical proof during a Bible study. Today she uses the Bible to counsel and teach other women on marriage and parenting.

Lance Tracy
3/26/1996

As a new Christian, Lance nearly got himself kicked out of his own home. Today he serves God by directing movies like "The Cross" and also leads Men in White, a purity ministry for men.

Leo Landaverde
06/10/1994

As a new Christian, Leo thought giving was a good idea that did not apply to him. Today he sits on the financial committee at Turning Point and has been blessed tremendously for his generosity.

Mike Upton
9/9/1984

When studying the Bible, Mike did not know what "sin" was, only that it was bad. Today he leads a community of believers at Turning Point and is an elder in training.

AUTHOR BIOGRAPHIES - The Maturing Process

Nicole Mencarini
2/16/2004
When studying the Bible, Nika got so heated that a girl thought she was going to punch her in the face. Today she peacefully serves God through her artistic and writing talents with InSpirit and Faith21.

Paul Hagerty
5/12/1996
As a new Christian, Paul told a girl that she liked him—on their first date. Today he produces plays and directs entertainment at Christian conferences. He also is married to someone who actually likes him.

Robert Noll
10/1/1989
As a new Christian, Robbie gave away almost everything he owned for spiritual reasons. Today he helps Christian artists through C.R.E.A.T.E., and makes sure his family has the posessions they need.

Shaela Druyon
2/4/2001
As a new Christian, Shaela once unthinkingly said "get behind me Satan" to a fellow believer. Today she teaches people about God's love through her writing and acting.

Shannon Milder
09/08/1999
As a new Christian, Shannon went home and zealously preached judgement to his family. Today he serves God through his music and speaks to his family in loving and understanding ways.

Susan Dindinger
7/31/1991
As a new Christian, Susie regularly confronted brothers on their sin. Today she helps people with loss as she leads a Grief Recovery ministry now spreading to many churches throughout the US.

Thomas Bundy
12/15/1991
As a new Christian, Tom was such a spiritual giant, he would stop to pray before eating candy bars. Today he serves in the marrieds ministry in his church and only prays over major meals.

Traci Minor
11/17/1993
As a new Christian, Traci asked how Jesus could relate to her if he had never been pregnant. Today she serves in the full time ministry at Turning Point helping moms and wives understand God's love.

AUTHOR BIOGRAPHIES - The Maturing Process

Tracy Taris
5/6/1997
As a new Christian, Tracy packed her calendar with good things in an attempt to pay for her salvation. Today she has a degree in psychology and uses her writing abilities with InSpirit and Faith21.

Vicki Hagadorn
10/23/1994
Vicki cancelled her baptism at 10:00 pm the night before. She finally did take the plunge, and today spends her life helping people find freedom in Christ through Grief Recovery and her writing.

Xochitl Wodrich
5/25/2001
As a new Christian, Xochitl confronted a brother on missing a church service. Today she writes for InSpirit and Faith21 and is happily married to the same man who still misses church due to work.

THANK YOU TO:

The Editors:
James Bean, Barbara Dindinger, Joseph Dindinger, Susan Dindinger, Ruth Doherty, Shaela Druyon, Darlene Bel Grayson, Kimba Henderson, Robin Parker, John Steinreich and Lindsay Walker.
Proofing by Curt Simmons and Toney Mulhollan.

The Layout & Graphics Team:
James DonVito, Paul Hagerty, Nicole Mencarini and Christian Vallejos, with help from Analucia Ordoñez.

Kevin and Tracena Holland for overseeing a ministry where a project like this would even be possible.

Tomi Kukta (www.boundonearth.com) for helping and guiding us through the whole process. And to all of you who encouraged us along the way.

To God, who inspired and encouraged us in this labor of love.

RESOURCES FROM IPI BOOKS

The Power of Gratitude

Gratitude is not just something nice to have. Gratitude is a pure and powerful expression of humility that transforms the mind and enriches the lives of those who see and feel it. Life has its negative elements, and many choose to focus on these with a complaining spirit. In a world where cynical and caustic comments seem to fill the air, some old-fashioned gratitude is badly needed.

In this insightful volume, Gordon Ferguson, a much-loved teacher and elder, shares lessons and examples from his own life. Some are heart warming, some are challenging. All of them help us to see ways in which we need to be grateful and show us the divine power that gratitude brings to our lives. This book brings into focus the life-changing power of gratitude that can change us to the core of our beings.

Price: $10.00 • 164 page softcover book • ISBN: 1577821246

Mine Eyes Have Seen the Glory
*The Victory of the Lamb
in the Book of Revelation*

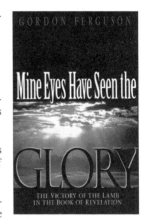

Mysterious. Confusing. Intriguing. Symbolic. Deep. Difficult. Literal. Futuristic. All these words and many others describe the final book of the Bible.

Misunderstood. Misinterpreted. Misapplied. These words speak of the "missed" message of Revelation in light of today's prevailing humanism, hedonism and hypocrisy.

Inspiring. Crucial. Radical. Victorious. Compelling. Challenging. Thrilling. Strengthening. These are a few of the right words—God's initial intent—about what is to happen in our hearts and in our souls after spending time with the apostle John on the island of Patmos as he reveals God through this revelation. In *Mine Eyes Have Seen the Glory*, Gordon Ferguson unlocks and unleashes God's powerful and timeless message—a message that will forever revolutionize our lives!

Price: $14.00 • 196 page softcover book • ISBN: 188453923

Available at www.ipibooks.com

RESOURCES FROM IPI BOOKS

Soul-ed Out
A Video Workshop for Devoted Living

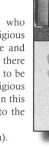

A recent study compared the lifestyles of those who claimed to be Christians and those who had no religious affiliation. Whether it was in the area of marriage and divorce, abortion, sexual immorality or integrity, there was no appreciable difference in those who claimed to be Christians and those who did not. It's obvious the religious world has lost touch with the genuine call of faith. In this powerful video series, Gordon calls listeners back to the meaning of making Jesus the Lord of their lives.

Four Video Lessons (approximately 1 hour each).

1. **Called Out**: *Exploring the significance and implications of being uniquely chosen by God.*

2. **Poured Out:** *How to make relationships that will help us change and change the world.*

3. **Sold Out:** *Why God desires total commitment to his Lordship and how to make that a reality in our lives.*

4. **Go Out:** *How to restore our love for the lost and help people become true disciples of Christ.*

Price: $12.00 • Four Hours (2 DVDS) • ISBN: 9780981737386

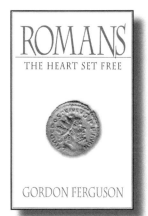

Romans
The Heart Set Free

Religion binds us. Grace and faith set us free. In large part, this is the message of the letter to the Romans. Considered by many to be Paul's greatest written work, Romans shows us the power of sin, the failure of normal religion to deal with it and the absolute victory we can have over it through faith in the blood that was shed on the cross.

In this book, Gordon Ferguson delves into what he believes just may be the most important book in Scripture. Gordon willl help you to understand the message of this great epistle as never before—and this understanding can set your heart free. What is more, once you get Romans, God gets you!

Price: $12.00 • 200 page softcover book • ISBN: 1577821688

Available at www.ipibooks.com

Illumination Publishers International

Toney Mulhollan has been in Christian publishing for over 30 years. He has served as the Production Manager for Crossroads Publications, Discipleship Magazine/UpsideDown Magazine, Discipleship Publications International (DPI) and on the production teams of Campus Journal, Biblical Discipleship Quarterly, Bible Illustrator and others. Toney serves as the Editor of Illumination Publishers International and Theatron Press. Toney is happily married to the love of his life, Denise Leonard Mulhollan, M.D. They make their home in Houston, Texas along with their daughter, Audra Joan.

For the best in Christian writing and audio instruction, go to the Illumination Publishers International website. We're commited to producing in-depth teaching that will inform, inspire and encourage Christians to a deeper and more committed walk with God. You can reach Toney Mulhollan by email at toneyipibooks@mac.com or at his office number, (832) 559-3658.

www.ipibooks.com